D0789811

INHERIT
THE EARTH

Other books by Gary North

Marx's Religion of Revolution, 1968
An Introduction to Christian Economics, 1973
Unconditional Surrender, 1981
Successful Investing in an Age of Envy, 1981
The Dominion Covenant: Genesis, 1982
Government by Emergency, 1983
The Last Train Out, 1983
Backward, Christian Soldiers?, 1984
75 Bible Questions Your Instructors
    Pray You Won't Ask, 1984
Coined Freedom: Gold in the Age of
    the Bureaucrats, 1984
Moses and Pharaoh, 1985
Negatrends, 1985
The Sinai Strategy, 1986
Unholy Spirits: Occultism and
    New Age Humanism, 1986
Conspiracy: A Biblical View, 1986
Honest Money, 1986
Fighting Chance, 1986 [with Arthur Robinson]
Dominion and Common Grace, 1987
Resurrection vs. Entropy, 1987
The Pirate Economy, 1987
Liberating Planet Earth, 1987
    (Spanish) *Teología de Liberación*, 1986

Books edited by Gary North

Foundations of Christian Scholarship, 1976
Tactics of Christian Resistance, 1983
The Theology of Christian Resistance, 1983
Editor, *Journal of Christian Reconstruction* (1974-1981)

INHERIT THE EARTH

Biblical Blueprints
for Economics

Gary North

Dominion Press
Ft. Worth, Texas

Copyright© 1987 by Gary North

All rights reserved. Written permission must be secured from the publisher to use or reproduce any part of this book, except for brief quotations in critical reviews or articles.

Published by Dominion Press
7112 Burns Street, Fort Worth, Texas 76118

Printed in the United States of America

Unless otherwise noted, all Scripture quotations are from the New King James Version of the Bible, copyrighted 1984 by Thomas Nelson, Inc., Nashville, Tennessee

Library of Congress Card Number 86-073075

ISBN 0-930462-56-4

This book is dedicated to
my four children:
Darcy, Scott, Lori, Caleb

TABLE OF CONTENTS

Part I
BLUEPRINTS

Social progress comes with the accumulation and development of *wealth*. Wealth comes, in a free economy, as a product of *work and thrift*—in short, of character. Capital is often accumulated by inheritance, a God-given right which is strongly stressed in the Bible. According to Proverbs 13:22, "A good man leaveth an inheritance to his children's children: and the wealth of the sinner is laid up for the just." Inheritance makes possible the accumulation not only of wealth within a family but of social power. Power is inescapable in any social order: it can either be concentrated in the state, or it can be allowed to flourish wherever ability makes it possible among the people. This decentralized wealth means also decentralized and independent power. Instead of a concentration of power in the state, there is instead a decentralization of power which moves in terms of varying and independent goals.

Again, in a free economy, *property* is freed from the restrictions of the state because it is under the restrictions of the family and of a religiously oriented community. In biblical law, there is no property tax, which means a basic and inalienable social security in the family and in property. The security of a man in his property, and in his inheritance, means a stability in the social order which is productive of progress.

R. J. Rushdoony*

---

*Rushdoony, *Politics of Guilt and Pity* (Fairfax, VA: Thoburn Press [1970] 1978), pp. 236-37.

INTRODUCTION

"The world economy is headed for a crash!"

"The economy has never been better!"

Well, which is it? We hear economists arguing both ways. How can we make up our minds? How should we prepare for the future? Is it a dark economic future or a bright one? The debate continues. Here are some familiar examples:

Western banks have loaned hundreds of billions of dollars to Third World nations that now are close to bankruptcy. Not only will they never repay their loans, but they are also borrowing heavily just to make their interest payments on time. If they default, the banks go bankrupt ("bankrupt" = bank + rupture). But they have to default; they don't have the money to repay.

But . . . Western technology is creating a totally new world, where computers will be cheap, and will perform tasks that are now barely dreamed of. We will work inside our homes, set our own schedules, and be able to buy computer-customized products at "off the rack" mass-production prices.

We are drowning in a sea of pollution. The great lakes are dying. Acid rain is rotting away our farms and businesses. Air pollution has become a way of life. Poisonous chemicals are everywhere; criminal syndicates are dumping them down our sewers and in our neighborhoods. Plastics never decompose. Nuclear energy leaves deadly wastes behind, and no one knows how to seal them up until they're harmless 100,000 years from now. We spend billions on health care, but we are dying of diseases that slowly destroy the body.

3

But . . . we are living longer than ever. Lake Erie has been cleaned up. Acid rain sometimes increases some kinds of agricultural output. Toxic wastes can be controlled. Nuclear power is safer than high pollution caused by high-waste, coal-fired power plants. Practical scientific solutions can be worked out. They always have been in the past. Don't worry.

The population boom threatens to overwhelm the world's resources. But . . . a falling birth rate in the industrial West points to racial and national extinction.

Americans can take advantage of the best educational opportunities in man's history. But . . . scores on academic tests dropped for 20 years, 1964-83, and only recently have turned up ever so slightly.

We have more drug addiction than ever before in our history. But . . . there is a revival of interest in religion among America's youth that we haven't seen before in this century.

Well, which is it? Is it the end of the world or the dawn of a new age?

Or is it just "business as usual"?

King Solomon's Day

Which was it in Solomon's day? The wisest king in the history of man was on the throne and was famous throughout the world (1 Kings 11). But he had 700 wives and 300 concubines (1 Kings 11:3). "So King Solomon surpassed all the kings of the earth in riches and wisdom" (1 Kings 10:23). "But King Solomon loved many foreign women . . ." (1 Kings 11:1).

King Solomon built God's temple (1 Kings 6). But "the Lord raised up an adversary against Solomon" (1 Kings 11:14a).

Wealth? "The king made silver as common in Jerusalem as stones" (1 Kings 10:27a). Taxes? Responded his son Rehoboam to tax protestors: "And now, whereas my father laid a heavy yoke on you, I will add to your yoke; my father chastised you with whips, but I will chastise you with scourges!" (1 Kings 12:11).

Solomon was the most militarily powerful king in Israel's history. But his son suffered a political revolt, the bulk of the kingdom split off and became independent, and Egypt (under king Shishak) invaded his land.

So what would you have said in Solomon's day? Were things doing well, or heading for a major crisis?

It was just about crisis time. But who knew for sure in Solomon's day? Only those who knew the Word of God, took it seriously, and looked at the world around them in terms of what the Bible says.

The Covenants of God

We examine our condition not simply by our present outward condition, but by the Word of God, the Bible. History is governed by God in terms of His eternal standards. God placed mankind under a covenant, the dominion covenant, and He told man that he must subdue the earth (Genesis 1:28).

What is a covenant? God comes before man and "lays down the law"—His law. Man must either conform to God and His law, or be destroyed. As He told Adam, "Eat of the tree of the knowledge of good and evil, and you will die." God deals with men as a king deals with his subjects. His covenant is to prosper us when we obey and curse us when we rebel.

God makes institutional covenants with men. There are three: family, church, and State. (I capitalize State when I refer to civil government in general. I don't capitalize it when I refer to the American political jurisdiction known as the states.) Each has an appropriate oath. Each has laws. Each has penalties for disobedience.

A Biblical covenant has five sections:

1. An announcement that God is *transcendent*—the supreme Creator and deliverer of mankind. God is completely superior to and different from men and the world He created. Yet He is also present with it: *immanent*.

2. The establishment of a *hierarchy* to enforce God's authority on earth.

3. A set of *rules* or laws man must follow in exercising his dominion over the earth. God will judge man by how well he follows these rules.

4. A list of *judgments* that will be imposed by God, who blesses man for obedience and curses man for disobedience.

5. A program of *inheritance*—a lawful transition that mortal men need in order to extend their dominion over creation.

We examine the laws of God, and we evaluate how well we are following them personally and with our own families. Then we compare the requirements of God's laws with institutions in our own nation: church, State, and family. If we find that society is disobeying God's covenantal principles, then we can conclude that *judgment is coming.* The curses of God will fall on those who rebel against Him.

Today's World

Today, the whole world is in rebellion against God in every area of life. This is just as true in the area of economics as it is in all the other areas of life.

This book talks about several principles of Biblical economics. I use the five-point covenantal scheme to divide up the chapters in Part One: two sets of five chapters each. What I argue is that these five points are *inescapable concepts.* We never face the question of "covenant or no covenant." We face the question: "*Whose* covenant?" God's covenant or man's covenant, a covenant with the Creator or a covenant with Satan: there are no other choices.

Christians are called by God to exercise dominion in every area of life. This includes economics. God has transferred the ownership of the world to Christians, just as He transferred it to Adam before Adam rebelled. We now are called to take possession of the world in terms of God's covenantal principles, and by means of God's sovereign grace.

This book is an introduction to a few of the themes of Biblical economics. It will demonstrate that God has established economic principles, and that men gain authority over the economy only by obeying these basic principles. Because men in general, and most Christians in particular, have adopted a different set of economic principles, we can expect judgment. We therefore need revival, meaning the restoration of God's economic principles.

If I am correct, then Christians must begin immediately to reconstruct their own lives, families, and churches before God's judgment on society begins. We must prove ourselves ready to lead. We do this by following God now, *before* judgment begins. Obedience to God's principles produces leadership. Disobedience to God's principles produces His judgment: man's disinheritance from God's riches.

If you don't want to be disinherited, either eternally or on earth, then start obeying God.

1

GOD OWNS THE WORLD

The earth is the Lord's, and all its fullness, The world and those who dwell therein. For He has founded it upon the seas, And established it upon the waters (Psalm 24:1-2).

I have four children. One thing I noticed very early is that there are certain concepts that come very easily to children. I think the second word all of them learned was "no!" This is understandable: my wife and I had taught them that word repeatedly — with appropriate instructional aids.

Another word they all learned incredibly fast was "mine!" I think it was their third word, except for my son Scott. It was his first word, if memory serves me rightly.

"Mine!" It comes so easily. It's as if the idea is implanted in little minds, all ready to come out as soon as they learn to talk. I think it *is* implanted in God's image-bearers.

What isn't so easy to teach them is the concept "yours." In fact, this may be one of the most difficult concepts of all to teach men. Wars are fought over it. Politicians are elected (or lose) in terms of it. People sometimes act as though there were no known limits on "mine," which therefore means there are no sure guarantees for "yours."

What do I mean, "mine"? What do you mean, "yours"? Does the Bible give us information that helps us to sort out these two opposite words?

His

Let's start at the beginning, the first chapter of the Book of Genesis. The very first verse announces, "In the beginning God created the heaven and the earth." That's clear enough. God is the Creator.

This brings us to the most important single doctrine of the Bible: the Creator-creature distinction. *There is a fundamental difference between the Creator and His creation.* This doctrine establishes that it is God and God alone who is the absolute ruler over the entire creation. God established the laws by which the creation operates, and He continually judges all the creation in terms of His law and His requirements. This is the doctrine of the *original creation*.

God created the world; therefore, He owns it. He is the absolute owner of everything. As we will see later on, He has delegated the ownership of the earth to mankind. The child is made in God's image (Genesis 1:26), and this is why it's so easy for a child to learn the concept "mine."

But God hasn't delegated everything to any one person, or any single institution. Sinful men may try to argue that God has delegated everything to the State (we call this economic doctrine "socialism"). Or they may act as though God gave everything to their favorite special-interest group. This is why "yours" is such a difficult idea to learn and teach. "Yours" means that whatever is mine is limited. Sinful men resent such a limitation.

But "mine" is always limited. "Mine" necessarily implies "yours." Only God is the absolute owner; only He owns everything. What He does, basically, is *lease* what He owns to men. Everything we own, including life itself, we owe to God. Each person will eventually be judged by how well he managed God's property.

Are we good stewards of God's property? How can we tell? Don't we have to make judgments concerning our honesty, our frugality, the wisdom of our decisions, and whether or not we have invested what God has entrusted to us wisely? Obviously, managing God's property implies *performance standards of ownership*. Where do we discover these standards? In the Bible.

Creation and Original Ownership

The first principle of a Biblical covenant is the principle of transcendence: God's absolute supremacy. God reigns supreme over everything. This means that He is high above the creation, and totally different from it. We deal with a sovereign God. In short, God runs the show.

This principle of transcendence relates to economics because ownership is ultimately *theocentric* (God-centered). He created all that exists, and He is at the center of the universe as its owner. *This means that ownership is ultimately a religious concept.* It cannot be properly understood without reference to God as the absolute owner of the creation. Similarly, it is impossible to discuss properly the responsibilities of ownership (which is what this book is all about) without also discussing what God specifically requires of men in their capacity as owners of property.

Providence

The doctrine of creation leads to a second doctrine, the doctrine of providence, meaning God's full-time maintaining and sustaining of the creation. God watches over and cares for the universe in a personal way. Not only did He create it, but He also sustains it. He makes certain that it continues through time, and it's solely through the power of God that the earth and the universe around it are sustained.

We read in the New Testament book, Colossians: "For by Him all things were created that are in heaven and that are on earth, visible and invisible, whether thrones or dominions or principalities or powers. All things were created through Him and for Him. And He is before all things, and in Him all things consist" (Colossians 1:16-17). The point is quite clear: God not only created the earth but He also sustains it. It is through His son Jesus Christ that history exists, that the world continues to operate. In short: *no God—no universe.*

God created and sustains everything. This is why David the Psalmist announced that it is God who is the owner of all the earth. The cattle on the thousand hills are His, and the thousand hills themselves are His (Psalm 50:10). There is nothing on earth that God does not absolutely, completely own. Because of this, we can rest assured that when we look to the Bible, we can find answers to the question: Who owns what?

One of the great debates which has separated societies in the twentieth century is the debate over the question of socialistic ownership versus private ownership. Socialists argue that the State (the civil government) should own the tools of production. In the 1930's, the National Socialists (Germany's Nazi Party) and the fascists in Italy argued that the State should *control* the tools of production, even though ownership was still officially private. In contrast, the free market is a system based on both the private ownership and private control of the tools of production.

Trinitarian Ownership

Which system of ownership does the Bible teach? We find the beginning of our answer in the doctrine of God, specifically, the New Testament doctrine of the Trinity, the union of God the Father, Christ the Son, and the Holy Spirit. When we accept the doctrine of the Trinity, which is the most basic new theological doctrine of New Testament Christianity, we have to recognize that God is at the same time many and one. There are *three persons* in the Trinity, but He is also *one God*.

His required system of ownership reflects His Trinitarian being. We discover that God sets forth rules of ownership that are at the same time *collective* and *individualistic*. Some pieces of property are owned by individuals; some are owned by families; other pieces of property are owned by associations and corporations; some are owned by churches, and some are owned by the civil government, meaning the State.

We also find in the Bible a system of *overlapping ownership*. Certain pieces of property are owned primarily by individuals but only secondarily by the State. In other cases, property will be owned by individuals, but families will also have rightful claims. In other words, property can never be defined as exclusively and absolutely owned by any single individual or any single human institution. This conclusion is implied by the very statement which begins this chapter: that God alone is the absolute owner of all the creation. He, and He alone, possesses absolute rights of ownership. All other ownership claims are subordinate.

When we speak of human ownership, we have to speak of God-given ownership. God is the absolute and ultimate ruler over all the creation, and therefore He is the absolute owner of the creation. We are told, however, that God has delegated to man the responsibility of caring for the creation (Genesis 1:28). Man is therefore a *steward* under the overall supervision of God. This means that man is responsible to God for all that he is, and he is responsible to God for the proper administration of everything that has been entrusted to him.

Private Ownership

There is no question concerning the Bible's affirmation of private property. This includes the New Testament. Jesus offered the following parable as a description of the kingdom of God. A land owner sends his servant out one morning to hire workers. Several are hired in the morning. The servant returns to the marketplace several times during the day. Each time, men agree to work in the fields. At the end of the day, the owner pays each of them the same wage. Those who worked all day complain. Why shouldn't they have received more money than those who came late?

What was Jesus trying to teach? That God saves some men early in their lives, some men in mid-life, and some men just before they die. Why should the early beneficiaries complain? They had sought employment, and they had received it. Had they not understood the terms? The land owner chides them: "Is it not lawful for me to do what I wish with my own things? Or is your eye evil because I am good?" (Matthew 20:15). Jesus compares the sovereignty of God in granting men salvation with the sovereignty of the owner over his goods.

The early church in Jerusalem practiced *voluntary* common ownership of goods. They had been warned by Jesus that Jerusalem would fall to the Romans (Luke 21), so they sold their goods while they still could, and shared their property.

A married couple, Ananias and Sapphira, sold a piece of property. They took some of the money aside, and gave the rest to the church. But they told the leaders that they had given all the proceeds of the sale to the church. Just before God judged them both with death for this sin of deception, Peter reminded Ananias: "While it remained, was it not your own? And after it was sold, was it not in your own control? Why have you conceived this thing in your heart? You have not lied to men but to God" (Acts 5:4).

Peter's point was clear: there is no required system of socialist or communist ownership in God's administration of things. Shared property is voluntary. Shared property was a *voluntary gift*, not a moral requirement, let alone a legal requirement.

Thus, one of the most popular arguments of "Christian" socialists, that the early church held property in common, is in fact an argument *against* State-required and State-enforced socialism. Only in Jerusalem did the church adopt this policy of shared property, for only Jerusalem was threatened with God's prophesied destruction. Yet a practice which was temporary and voluntary has been used by evil men to defend a permanent and involuntary system of theft by ballot box, modern socialism and the welfare State.

Ownership as a Social Function

Ownership is a social function. Most people don't understand this. Capitalism's critics certainly don't. When the critics think of private ownership, they think of a greedy, grasping, profit-seeking, tight-fisted owner of property who uses his property exclusively for his own personal self-advancement. They think of the capitalist as Ebenezer Scrooge.

This has been the traditional cartoon version of the capitalist in all socialist parties. The capitalist is seen as an exploiter. He is seen as someone whose plans must be thwarted by the community as a whole, acting politically through the State, in order that the community's interests can be upheld.

This is a complete misunderstanding of private property. Individuals own property as a dual stewardship: first before God, and second for the community. Understand: I didn't say that people hold property for the benefit of the *State*. The State is not the same as the community (though proponents of Big Government seldom mention this). People don't hold property primarily to benefit the civil government, meaning that political and bureaucratic institution which God has established to punish evildoers. Ownership in the Bible and also in a free market isn't primarily a *State* function. I am arguing instead that ownership is a *social* function, and that men must divide up property according to the needs and demands of the community as a whole, *if owners wish to be wise investors and receive the highest profits and benefits from their property.*

In short, the State is not the same as the community. The community is a lot broader than the State: it is made up of families, churches, schools, businesses, and voluntary associations of all kinds. The officials of the State legally represent the community in Biblically limited ways: they offer protection of life and property (Exodus 22), trials by jury (Exodus 18; Romans 13:1-7), national defense (Judges), medical quarantine (Leviticus 13, 14), and public safety (Exodus 21:28-36).

A Piece of Land

Let's see how the social function of ownership operates in practice. Say that an individual holds a piece of land. This land can be used for many purposes: farming, a site for a factory, a site for a school, a site for homes or apartment houses, etc. In other words, *the land has more than one use*, and therefore the individual owner has to decide the best possible way to use the land.

If he is a profit-seeking owner, he must ask himself this question: "What do people in the community want me to do with my property?" To answer this question, he needs to determine the possible rate of return, either from selling the property or renting it out. In order to receive the highest profits from the land, he needs to use it to produce whatever people value the most, as determined by their willingness to pay. The normal rule used by a seller to determine what the community (participants in the market) really wants is this: *high bid wins*. The economy is essentially a giant auction.

Let's say that an individual decides that his property should be used either to build an apartment house or to grow food. People want living space, and an apartment complex is a way in which people can get inexpensive living space. By using the land as a site for the construction of an apartment complex, the owner makes it impossible for the land to be used for growing food. He denies other users access to the property. This is the essence of all ownership: *denying access to an asset*. It is the legal ability to say, "This use, not that one." Such a decision should always be made in terms of this principle: "I'm responsible."

What if a farmer also wants this property? What economic incentives can the farmer offer to the land owner to persuade him that he, the farmer, should be allowed to take control of the property? Obviously, the best way for him to do it would be to offer the owner a lease or a rental payment or even cash on the line in order to gain exclusive use of the property.

In this example, one group of consumers benefits, and a different group loses. Some consumers are more interested in increasing the supply of apartment house space, thereby making space cheaper, while others are more concerned with increasing the supply of food, and thus making food cheaper.

The apartment house builder acts as a middleman for the people who want to rent the space. Similarly, the farmer acts as a middleman for people who want to buy food cheaply. Each group of consumers is represented, *economically speaking*, by an agent. He is not a legal agent, but he is an economic agent. He does not hold a piece of paper signed by all the members of the group that says: "This man is our lawfully designated representative." He is simply a person who is willing to put his own money (or money he has borrowed and is responsible for) on the line *in the hope of selling the property's economic output to the special interest group that he believes will pay him the highest price*. The builder and the farmer each want to sell or rent the use of the land to "his" group of consumers, not because he knows them, but because he believes they are willing to bid the highest for the property in the competitive auction we call the free market.

The number-one economic question is this: Who will offer the highest bid? Will it be the *consumers of food*, or will it be the *consumers of living space*? The owner of the land is rewarded to act as a steward (property manager) for those people in the community who are willing to pay the most for the land. If he refuses to follow this rule, he cannot gain the maximum economic return from that property. The important point is that the future profit he expects to make from the sale of the land is his *economic signal from future consumers* that they want him to sell it to the highest bidding buyer.

Assume that the farmer (the "agent" of future food buyers) is unwilling to bid as much for the property as the "agent" of the future apartment house dwellers. The man who presently owns the property nevertheless allows the farmer to lease or buy the property at the lower price. He makes money from the sale of the land to the farmer, but to do this, he must give up the money that the apartment house builder would have paid for the land. He suffers a financial loss: he loses the money he could have made by selling to the apartment house builder, *minus* the money he actually made by selling to the farmer.

There is nothing very amazing about this analysis of how the free market works. It is a giant auction. The average person understands this process, even if he has never thought much about it. All this analysis says is: "You can't get something for nothing." We live in a world of scarcity. Scarcity means that if every item were sold at zero price, there would be more demand than supply. So we put prices on such items in order to limit demand. We decide who gets what by a system of bidding, just like an auction. To get one thing, a person must give up something else. And most of the time, we make our decisions based on the rule: *high bid wins*. We do the best we can with what we've got. But what is "the best"? We search out "the best" by asking ourselves: "What is the best (highest) price I can get for this item or service?"

Ownership Isn't Free

The owner has the legal right to do what he wants with his property, but he cannot escape the economic consequences of his decision. In other words, we can say that he is free to sell his property, but ownership is not free. Ownership bears costs. *Ownership is expensive.* Make a mistake by selling too low, and you suffer the economic consequences. To get the most income as a seller, you need to listen to the agent of those consumers who the agent expects in the future to pay the highest price. This is the agent who will pay you the highest price in order to take control of the property. In this case, you need to listen to future renters and not to future eaters.

By what standard should an individual make a decision as to how to use his property? There are many answers to this: to benefit a particular special-interest group, or an organization, or a particular group of consumers in the community, or the political authorities, or any number of other possible buyers and users of the property. But a very important factor in allowing an individual to make a choice as to what use the property will be put is the question of *profit or loss.*

The property owner has the legal right to subsidize (assist financially) a particular group by selling that property at a below-market price, but he can't do this free of charge. By selling the property at a price that is below the price another buyer would otherwise bid, *the seller personally bears the loss.* What loss? The money he forfeits because he is selling below market. In effect, he makes a *gift* to the buyer of the difference between the normal market price and the actual selling price. There is nothing morally wrong with making this sort of a gift, but the gift cannot be made free of charge. There are no free gifts, just as there are no free lunches. (Even the free gift of God's grace to mankind in Jesus Christ had to be paid for: at the cross.)

Who else suffers a loss? All those consumers who wanted their "agent" to buy the property at the higher price, but who couldn't get the seller to cooperate. But these thwarted consumers have the satisfaction of knowing that the seller bore a financial loss because of his decision. If they lose, then at least he loses, too.

The Auction

How does society convince individuals to meet the needs of the largest and most productive segments of that society? It does it through *competitive bidding*. Ownership, therefore, is very much like a giant auction: the high bid normally wins. Even when the high bid doesn't win, the *known* high bid always makes itself felt in the actual decision of the seller.

The seller must decide whether he wants more money, or more satisfaction from giving all or a portion of that property to a particular individual or group. But the social function of ownership cannot be escaped. Hour by hour, minute by minute, the individual who owns a piece of property gives up all of the income he otherwise could have received if he had just sold the property or put it to some other use.

There is no escape from this process. The market makes itself felt every moment of the day because of the *income which is lost* from all competing uses of the property. In the mind of the property owner, the benefits received from a particular use of the property offset these losses.

Theocentric Ownership

I have already said that all ownership is given by God and guided by God. All ownership is therefore *providential*. Ownership is therefore *theocentric*. God is at the center of all ownership. This has important economic implications.

Man's Limited Knowledge

One of the characteristics of God is that He knows everything there is to know. He is *omniscient* (all-knowing). Before time began, God knew everything that is taking place today, and He knows everything that will take place in the future (Ephesians 1). There is nothing in the universe that takes place that God is not

completely aware of. Knowing everything is the completely unique
ability of God. This ability cannot be transferred to any creature.
There are secret things known only to God (Deuteronomy 29:29).

Because of this fact of mental life, men cannot truly claim to
know everything, either as individuals or as members of a com-
mittee. They cannot honestly claim to know every possible use to
which a property might be put. They cannot honestly claim to
know the very best possible use of that property. They make esti-
mations. They make guesses. They do their best to determine
where they can get the highest rate of return on their capital. But
ultimately, they can never know for certain whether or not they
are putting their property to the most profitable use, or the most
socially beneficial use, or the most morally beneficial use. This is
why *the ownership of property is always a moral responsibility*. It's a burden as well as a benefit.

Biblical Law

Where do we go for guidance concerning which kinds of property should be owned by individuals, and which kinds of property
should be owned by other associations or agencies? Where do we
find the best guidelines ("blueprints")?

Answer: we must look to Biblical law. When we examine what
God has revealed to us about Himself and His creation, we find
guidelines ("blueprints") concerning the proper distribution of
property. We find guidelines for the private ownership of property, for the inheritance of property, for the support of the poor,
for the support of the civil government, and so forth. If we don't
turn to the Bible and to Biblical law in order to discover these
answers, then we get ourselves tangled up in fruitless, God-
dishonoring debates between rival humanistic political and economic philosophies. Throughout history, there have been endless
debates over "private ownership versus collective ownership."
These debates have not been resolved, simply because men do not
agree about their most basic beliefs. They do not share a common
moral viewpoint. They disagree about where the universe came
from or who controls it. They therefore disagree with each other

concerning the origin of property and the standards of ownership. They disagree concerning stewardship. They have not been able to come to any agreed-upon conclusions concerning who owns what, and who *should* own what.

This little book represents an attempt to clarify some of these fundamental issues. No brief book could possibly cover all of the important topics, but at least it can serve as a general introduction. There is no doubt that what the Bible teaches about the ownership of property is opposed to modern socialist economic theories and also opposed to theories of absolute private property. But on the whole, we find that God has delegated more responsibilities to private associations, especially the family, than He has delegated to the civil government and to its bureaucratic agencies.

Conclusion

The Biblical concept of ownership is centered in God. "For every beast of the forest is Mine, And the cattle on a thousand hills" (Psalm 50:10). God is the absolute owner of all the creation, and He sustains it by means of His supreme ruling power.

He established man as a manager over His property, and He has laid down laws for the administration and transfer of property that must be obeyed if this work is to be profitable. They are to be faithful stewards to God. Private property is not an absolute rule, and neither is State-owned property. But as we shall see, most property in the Bible is not owned or controlled by either the civil government or the church. Most property is owned by *families or the economic agents of families.*

All ownership is social. Buyers and sellers compete—buyers against buyers, and sellers against sellers—for the scarce resources of the creation. This competitive process, which some economists call a *process of discovery*, places economic pressures on owners to administer their property for the benefit of consumers.

Legally, the Bible allows great freedom of private property management, but from an economic point of view, every decision (or lack of decision) on the part of the owner bears its appropriate cost. Any property owner who refuses to meet consumer demand thereby loses income, or loses an increase in the value of his property, or both. He pays a price for ignoring consumer demand. He is generally *legally free* to do what he chooses with his property, so long as he does not injure (physically or morally) any other person; he cannot use his property *free of charge*.

We must begin our study of Biblical economic principles by assuming the following beliefs:

1. God is the supreme Creator.
2. God is the absolute owner of all property.
3. God declared that man should rule over (have dominion over) the other creatures of the earth.
4. God gives man the responsibility of property management (stewardship before God).
5. Ownership is a social function (stewardship before men).
6. God has established standards for legal ownership.
7. God has established laws for man's management of God's property.
8. Biblical law reveals these standards.
9. Man, unlike God, has limited knowledge.
10. Profit-and-loss standards help men discover the best use of the property which God has entrusted to them.
11. The free market economy is a giant auction.
12. The normal rule of this giant auction is "high bid wins."
13. The middleman is the *economic agent* of consumers.
14. Biblical law establishes the proper rules of ownership and administration of property.

2

DOMINION BY SUBORDINATION

Then God said, "Let Us make man in Our image, according to Our likeness; let them have dominion over the fish of the sea, over the birds of the air, and over the cattle, over all the earth and over every creeping thing that creeps on the earth." So God created man in His own image: in the image of God He created him; male and female He created them. Then God blessed them, and God said to them, "Be fruitful and multiply; fill the earth and subdue it; have dominion over the fish of the sea, over the birds of the air, and over every living thing that moves on the earth" (Genesis 1:26-28).

The second principle of a Biblical covenant is *the principle of hierarchy-authority*. God directly and personally controls His creation (principle one: transcendence). Nevertheless, God, the sovereign owner who created the universe, has delegated to mankind the full responsibility of caring for the creation as a whole. God doesn't directly control the earth apart from those He has chosen to manage His property. He directly controlled all of it during the first week of creation, but He no longer does. In His providential control and mercy, He has decided to delegate control over His property to mankind throughout history.

In order to restrain each person, and also to give him the increased productivity that is made possible by cooperative efforts (1 Corinthians 12), God has established several hierarchical chains of command through which men are to exercise their God-given authority. The three God-ordained hierarchies are family, church, and State. All three are governments. All three are marked by

23

oaths before God. All three are *bottom-up* systems of appeals courts, especially the church and State. Christian maturity increases when individual *self-government under God's law* increases.

This raises a whole series of very difficult questions. The most important question is: What or who is the primary manager of God's property?

Family Property

There can be little doubt that the Bible teaches that property is primarily owned by families. In the same sense that God is Himself a family of three persons, so is mankind. Mankind reproduces itself and extends dominion over the creation through the most universal institutional unit, the family. God placed Adam and Eve under the terms of the dominion covenant as a family. He told them to be fruitful and multiply — a biological task to be performed within the bounds of the family covenant. It is certainly not a bureaucratic task given to church or State. Families therefore are the primary owners of property because the family is the primary agency of dominion. Of course, the family never operates independently from the civil government. Whenever it unlawfully tries to do so, it becomes a tyrannical local civil government. But the family is the primary agency of dominion, not church or State.

Because of the God-imposed division of labor principle (1 Corinthians 12), we need cooperation. But we need it not just with fellow church members. How can we get cooperation from the non-Christian world? Through our ability to offer economic incentives to them. This is why the economy is the primary means of cultural dominion: it enables Christians to enlist the skills and capital of those who do not agree with our first principles of life. They cooperate with us in order to further their ends, yet their activities ultimately extend the kingdom of God in history.

In the Old Testament, property was unquestionably familistic, and families had very definite responsibilities for the long-term care and administration of the land that was placed under their control. In principle, this has not changed in New Testament times. While we no longer own property through membership in one of twelve tribes (Numbers 36), as the ancient Israelites did, we nevertheless own property as stewards for families.

Individual Ownership

Does this mean that private individuals who are not married and who have never been married are not entitled to own property? No, because they are still *heads of households*. It does mean, however, that individuals are responsible for the care of parents in those cases where the parents are unable to care for themselves (Exodus 20:12). It also means that the unmarried individual has to make decisions concerning who will inherit the property. He therefore must act in the name of some other family or some other institution with respect to the inheritance. If he refuses to choose a lawful heir, then the State steps in at his death and decides who will inherit. There is therefore no escape from the responsibility of managing property. Someone will inherit. (See Chapter Five: "Inheritance.")

It's obvious that most individuals eventually marry and have families. In the book of Genesis, we read that a man removes himself from the control of his parents when he marries, by setting up an independent family unit which is no longer ruled by the original family (Genesis 1:24).

Most individuals say that they would give up almost anything for the sake of their families. Most men would claim that they are working in order to advance the social status or the economic status or the educational status of their families. There is no question that in most cases, a man who is married will have different interests and a different sense of responsibility than an unmarried man normally possesses.

Studies have indicated that married men live longer than unmarried men, that they are less likely to commit crimes than unmarried men, and that they are less likely to become social misfits than unmarried men. Marriage leads to stability, prosperity, and predictable moral behavior. Without strong family units, a society will be far poorer, and in most cases, each individual within society would find himself with much less wealth.

In other words, goods and services flow in the direction of those who take *personal responsibility* over their own affairs, and over the affairs of those individuals whom God has made dependent on them for a period of time. As the Bible says, "But the wealth of the sinner is stored up for the righteous" (Proverbs 13:22b).

Individuals possess ownership rights, meaning the *human right* lawfully to exclude others from controlling a particular piece of property. Never forget: humans possess rights to property. *Property rights are therefore really human rights*. The popular slogan, "human rights are more important than property rights," is just that, a slogan. It is frequently a highly misleading slogan. It is almost always used to increase the power over property by State bureaucracies at the expense of families. Individuals are usually members of families, and family units have important legal claims over individuals, and therefore over property. But this means that families therefore possess God-given property rights to exclude the State.

Each of God's three lawfully ordained human governments—family, church, and State—possesses God-given authority in the field of economics, but the primary agency of economic authority is the family. The family is the primary agency of dominion, and dominion involves the extension of man's authority over the various operations of the creation.

Autonomy and Impotence

Individuals are judged by their performance of required obligations before God and before other men. People's actions and words have meaning precisely because there is a God who created them, sustains them, and carefully guides and cares for the world in which men operate. The world has meaning because there is a *plan of God* and also a set of *ethical standards* that God has established. The world and the life of the individual have meaning only because both the world and individuals are under God's guidance and rule.

This means that built into creation is a concept of authority. God is the ruler over His creation. Men must answer to God and be responsible to Him. *The basis of any man's rule over the creatures and the resources of the earth is his humility and his willing obedience to a sovereign and all-knowing God.* This is what Jesus meant when He announced: "Blessed are the meek, For they shall inherit the earth" (Matthew 5:5). He meant *meek before God.* He did not mean "wimps before men." He meant just the opposite. We need *humility* to take *authority.*

Grabbing for Power

When men forget this and act as though they were *independent rulers* over the earth, they tend to lose power over time. This is one of the ironies of history, for when Adam rebelled against God, he was trying to assert his own control over the creation. Men rebel against God and God's moral standards in order to increase their own power. This rebellion backfires.

When men depart from the God who created them and who sustains them and the universe, they leave the one source of long-term power and authority which is given to man. What I'm arguing, in short, is that men will either be *under God* and exercise dominion *over the creation*, or else they will attempt to ignore God and therefore find themselves increasingly controlled by the creation (including other men).

God-hating people may say that they are working to take power over the creation, but such an effort means that certain individuals are trying to take control over all the rest of us. When "man takes control of man," this means that a power-grabbing elite is attempting to take control of everybody else.

Individuals and groups that attempt to control other people in defiance of God's laws always find resistance. They involve themselves in wars, assassinations, struggles for power, and all of the sorts of crises that take place when men forget God, ignore His law, and attempt to impose their own will without any kind of restraint.

Moses and Pharaoh

We see a very good example of this power-seeking in the attempt of the Pharaoh of Moses' day to maintain control over the Hebrew slaves. When Moses came before him to challenge him to

allow the Hebrews to go on a three-day journey in order to sacrifice to their God, Pharaoh responded by asking rhetorically, "Who
is the Lord, that I should obey His voice to let Israel go? I do not
know the Lord, nor will I let Israel go" (Exodus 5:2). Other
tyrants who lorded themselves over the Israelites in later years
would utter similar arrogant challenges to God.

Why did the people of Israel find themselves in bondage?
Because God tells all men that whenever they forget that He is the
source of all man's benefits—that He is the supreme ruler over
creation—they will eventually find themselves in slavery. When
men *forget God*, they thereby *forget liberty*. People who rebel against
the God of the Bible will always find themselves placed under the
ruling power of some imitation god.

The repeated defeats and captivities of the Hebrews came
because they repeatedly rebelled against God. God told them, in
effect, "If you choose to worship another god, I will give you over
to the power of that foreign god which you chose to worship." This
happened again and again. It led to dictatorship over the
Hebrews by kings and pharaohs and tyrants who worshipped the
other gods—gods that the Hebrews had "run away" to worship.
When men run away from God, they run into bondage. Foreign tyrants
over Israel often claimed to be the actual physical image or representative of these other gods, and they could therefore easily control the Hebrews, because the Hebrews could no longer appeal to
the God of the Bible they had denied when they worshipped other
gods.

In effect, what God was saying to them was this: "So you want
to worship other gods? Fine, go ahead and worship them. Let Me
give you a taste of what those other gods *really* are. Let Me show
you the kind of society which is created by people who worship
that sort of foreign deity. Let Me show you what it's like to serve
politicians and bureaucrats who have rebelled against Me in the
name of that god." Even if that god is *Man*.

We are either under the God of the Bible, or we are under
some other god. It's not possible for men to escape serving some
higher authority. The question is: *Which* authority? Will men

serve the loving God who created them, or will they serve a creation of their own minds (Romans 1:18-23)? Will they serve the personal God of the Bible, or will they serve some tinhorn dictator, or some tyrannical political party, or some warlord, or some other fake god who struts across the face of the earth and over the backs of the broken bodies of men?

Authority and Obedience

What the doctrine of dominion teaches is that there is a *chain of command* in the universe. God, as the creator of the universe, controls everything that happens in that universe. He sits on His throne as the Judge of the universe, and it is He who decides who has met His standards and who has violated them. God is the Judge. We are the judged.

God controls the universe and asserts His sovereignty over man. Men, as representatives of this sovereign God, possess God-given authority over the creation. God is a lawful God, and He has established moral and other kinds of laws over His creation. As God's image, man is able to understand these laws and apply them. Man, as a sovereign agent — an agent operating under the rule of God — serves as a *miniature judge*, a representative of God's supreme authority (1 Corinthians 6:3). He doesn't have final authority, but does have *legitimate delegated authority*; the authority God has given him to make wise decisions here on earth.

When Adam rebelled in the garden against God, one of the curses that was placed on him was that the agricultural produce of the field would begin to bring up weeds and other kinds of undesirable growth (Genesis 3:18). Animals also became a threat to man, and it was only after the great Flood in Noah's day that God placed the fear of man in the hearts of the animals (Genesis 9:2). Man learned what it meant to suffer rebellion.

Insubordination

Adam rebelled against the authority of God, and then nature rebelled against the authority of Adam. Adam learned what it was like to govern insubordinate individuals who do their best (worst) to refuse to submit themselves to God's supreme guidance by refusing to submit to man's guidance. He also learned what it was like to suffer death. Adam's dominion over the earth was interrupted by sickness and then by death. Why? Because Adam had attempted to assert his role as the judge between the truth of God's Word and the truth of Satan's word. But there is only one supreme judge, and that judge is God.

It has become far more difficult for man to exercise dominion on earth because of the results of Adam's rebellion. Sinful men find that the world around them is in perpetual rebellion against them. Sinful rulers also find that their followers are stubborn and resistant to their commands. Some of them are even willing to revolt against him. The more that individuals try to assert the power of God, which is not theirs to possess, the more they produce resentment and rebellion in the men under their authority.

This doesn't mean that all authority is wrong. It simply means that all God-defying, *lawless* authority is wrong.

Multiple Hierarchies

Just as God rules over creation, there will always be men who exercise authority over other men. There will always be ranking chains of command, but any attempt to set up a single chain of command is demonic, for no human institution possesses absolute authority. There are rulers of church and State. There are rulers in business affairs. There are rulers in clubs, non-profit associations and other voluntary groups of many different kinds. In organized sports there are captains, and there must be a coach. There must also be a referee.

Christians understand that they are in a very real sense spiritual soldiers. They should also realize that like any good soldier, *each Christian is under someone else's authority.* Obedience to superior authority is the testing ground of future authority and future responsibility. We begin as followers, not as leaders.

God judges a man by how well he performs his task under the authority of some other person. Depending on how well he performs under this authority, he should or should not become a leader of other individuals. This is true in families, in businesses, and in military operations. It's true in every area of life. Authority over others is always by rank. Authority over others is always by covenant (a legally binding interpersonal bond under God: church, State, or family) or contract (a legally binding agreement among people). Every covenant or contract requires men to submit themselves to the authority of some ruling agent, if only the enforcing authority.

The Trinity

Christianity teaches that there are three persons in the Godhead. Each person is equal in honor and majesty, power, and glory, yet each of the persons has a different function with respect to mankind and the creation. Throughout His career, Jesus affirmed that He was simply doing the will of His Father, from His youth (Luke 2:49) to His death (Matthew 26:39). This does *not* mean that Jesus was inferior to God the Father in terms of His *being*; it simply means that He was subordinate in His *function* in relationship to God, meaning subordinate in His activities with respect to the church and the creation in general. Jesus' submission to the Father's authority in history doesn't imply moral inferiority or inferiority in terms of His being. (It is always a sign of false theology when the inferiority of Jesus is proclaimed, in contrast to His subordinate functional status in history under God the Father.)

We also find that the Holy Ghost is sent by both the Father (John 14:26) and the Son (John 16:7) to minister unto mankind. In other words, the Holy Ghost is under the authority of both the Father and the Son. This also does *not* mean that the Holy Ghost is inferior in His being to the Father and the Son. It means only that He is under Their authority in His relationship to history.

If two of the very persons of the Godhead are not jealous of the Father, neither should men be jealous of lawful authority.

The Family

Husbands are to exercise godly, responsible dominion, and they are to take responsibility for the actions of the members of their families, precisely because heads of households are God's designated agents on earth with respect to family members (Ephesians 5:22-33; 6:1-4; 1 Peter 3:1-7). Husbands are to follow God's laws. Their authority is not independent of God's. They are under the authority of God and other institutions, whether church, State, business, or charity.

There is also a hierarchy of responsibility and authority within the human family. Wives are under the authority of their husbands. This doesn't mean that wives are in any way morally inferior to their husbands. In many cases, wives may be far superior ethically to their husbands. Nevertheless, they are to obey them so that they may learn to exercise authority in their own households. Exercising proper authority requires submission to proper authority. In short, *dominion requires subordination.* If wives wish to exercise responsible authority in other areas of life, they must become obedient to their husbands, just as husbands must become obedient to God, the church, and the State. To lead, you must first follow. People don't start out as generals in an army—not if that army is going to defeat another army, anyway.

By denying this fundamental principle, the "women's liberation movement" has done more to remove long-term authority from women than any other intellectual and political movement of this century. We see this clearly in the case of "no-fault divorce." Recent studies indicate that within one year after such a divorce, the former wife's overall economic status falls by over 70%. This is liberation? No; it is a form of bondage.[1] All rebellion against God and God's standards results in bondage.

Women are not to be doormats. Nobody is supposed to be a doormat. They advance their status and authority by helping their husbands and children. If they possess the grace and wisdom to become economically productive without ceasing to assist husbands and children, they should do so (Proverbs 31). They advance their family's fortunes and authority by serving husbands, children, employers, and therefore consumers.

---

1. Sylvia Ann Hewett, *A Lesser Life: The Myth of Women's Liberation in America* (New York: Morrow, 1986).

Dominion is by service. Dominion is by subordination. *Dominion is by covenant.* "Authority over" is achieved by "submission to." Authority is therefore achieved by following established laws. The question is: *Whose laws will men affirm?* God's, or someone else's? The question is: *Whose covenant?*

God has created a whole series of responsible human institutions. No single institution has absolute authority over any other institution. Certainly, no single institution has absolute authority over all other institutions. Any such assertion of absolute authority is a challenge to the doctrine of the sovereignty of God, and it leads, inescapably, to tyranny.

The State

In our generation it has been the State above all other institutions which has asserted this kind of all-encompassing authority over men. To the extent that men have believed such a doctrine of the supremacy of the State, they have placed themselves under other men whose sins, whose ignorance, whose errors, and whose lack of good judgment will lead them all into a ditch. The Bible speaks of the blind leading the blind into the ditch (Luke 6:39). When State bureaucrats, planners, and politicians lead all the rest of us into the ditch, everyone suffers.

What the Bible teaches us, in other words, is a system of multiple hierarchies and multiple authorities, all under the overall sovereignty of God. When men are self-governed — when men exercise self-government under God in terms of God's revealed law — we find that the State, the church, and other powerful institutions are limited. But when men assert autonomous (self-made law) sovereignty over their own affairs, thereby denying the sovereignty of God above them, we find that societies are torn apart by conflicts between groups that insist on anarchy — a Stateless society — and rival groups that insist on a totalitarian State. Men are governed either by people who covenantally represent God and God's law, or they will be governed by other men who represent some other god and that god's law.

Authority: Top-Down or Bottom-Up?

The basis of dominion is cooperation under God. Every institution needs to have a specified chain of command or chain of responsibility, so that men understand and accept: (1) their God-imposed limits, (2) their God-given assignments, (3) their personal responsibility for the resources that God provides them with, meaning (4) the God-established standards for judging performance which the organization enforces over its members.

Without these guidelines ("blueprints"), men cannot make wise economic decisions. They cannot decide what to do and when to do it. A society without hierarchies is impossible — a myth. Any society that did not have many groups that have internal ranks of authority would rest on a foundation of chaos. Societies cannot survive without hierarchies. *Hierarchy is an inescapable concept.* It's never a question of "hierarchy vs. no hierarchy"; it's always a question of which hierarchy or hierarchies.

Nevertheless, Biblical Christianity never asserts that any single authority is absolutely supreme, except the Creator God. This means that there must be God-ordained and God-limited institutions to settle disputes. It also means that *there should be no central planning agency over the entire economy.*

The Biblical concept of social order is not a top-down pyramid of political power, but rather a bottom-up system of appeals courts. Initiative should normally begin at the lower level of the social system. (An exception, obviously, is during wartime. Yet even here, most of the details for carrying out any mission must be dealt with at the platoon level.)

Vladimir Lenin, the Communist revolutionary who captured Russia in 1917, was a master of tyrannical, pyramid-like organization. He once contrasted his "revolutionary political democracy" (the Bolshevik Party) with the less centralized socialists, the Social Democrats: "The latter want to proceed from the bottom upwards. . . . The former proceed from the top. . . . My idea . . . is 'bureaucratic' in the sense that the Party is built from the top downwards. . . ." He transformed Russia into the Soviet Union in terms of this blueprint. It is demonic to the core.

Conclusion

God has entrusted to mankind the administration of the earth. We are to do all things to the glory of God. We are to submit ourselves to the law of God. The law is our tool of authority, and the law is the standard God will use to judge us on the final day. Therefore, as responsible agents, we must govern ourselves and all those over whom we have been given lawful authority. We are to govern ourselves in terms of the same law-order that we expect the final judgment to bring over us (Matthew 7:1).

Those people who are graciously chosen by God to become His adopted children (John 1:12)—those who have publicly declared their belief in Jesus Christ as the only acceptable sacrifice which satisfies the eternal wrath of God, and who are covenanted to (under the discipline of) a local church—are no longer under the *curse* of God's law. But they don't deny their need for the law's *protection*. They want God's protection, which necessarily means that they want Biblical law's protection. This means that they want protection *by* lawfully established institutions that are based on and restrained by God's revealed law. They want protection *from* those institutions that deny that they are under God's authority and God's law. They want freedom under God and God's law; they want to avoid tyranny under some other god and some other law.

In short, Christians are supposed to recognize that *authority is inescapable,* and therefore that *hierarchy is inescapable.* It's always a question of *whose* authority and *what kind of* hierarchy.

To understand the nature of responsible ownership before God, we need to acknowledge these Biblical principles:

1. Men are responsible primarily to God.
2. God is the only true central planner.
3. The primary agency of economic planning is the family, as the primary owner of property.
4. The primary agent of the family is the husband.
5. Socialistic central planning is demonic; it is man's attempt to replace God.

6. Socialistic central planning requires a tyrannical elite.

7. Individual responsibility requires individual initiative.

8. Individual initiative requires personal liberty.

9. Obedience to God is the basis of liberty.

10. Reconciling differences requires a system of appeals courts (plural).

11. Men are responsible (subordinate) to several human agencies.

12. No one human institution is absolutely sovereign.

13. Submission to authority is absolutely necessary. Man must serve someone.

14. Leadership begins with "followership."

15. Man operating independently from God (autonomy) results in failure and defeat.

16. Wealth flows toward those who accept personal responsibility for their actions.

17. Responsible action requires a concept of law and ethics.

18. Biblical law is the basis of responsible dominion.

3

THEFT

You shall not steal (Exodus 20:15).

The third principle of a Biblical covenant is *the principle of ethics-dominion*. The basis of long-term authority is obedience to God's law. This principle of *dominion through moral obedience* is related to economics in numerous ways, but nothing is clearer than the Bible's prohibition against theft. The eighth commandment (seventh, if you're a Lutheran) prohibits theft. This unquestionably is the basis of a defense of the idea of private property.

More important, as we learn in the tenth commandment, God's law requires the protection of family property. The tenth commandment prohibits coveting anything that is our neighbor's. It prohibits the mental origin of grasping, greedy evil. The eighth commandment prohibits theft—a visible manifestation of this coveting process. It establishes for all time that it's illegal and immoral for an individual to steal property which belongs to someone else. As we shall see, it's equally illegal in God's sight to get the State to steal for you. The commandment doesn't say, "You shall not steal, except by majority vote."

Stolen Fruit

The most important single example of theft that we have in the Bible is the theft by Adam and Eve of the fruit of the tree of the knowledge of good and evil (Genesis 3). God set a legal boundary around that tree. He told them that they could eat from any tree in the garden, with the exception of this one tree (Genesis

37

2:16-17). The test of men's responsibility under God was visibly a test of respect for another's property. Would they allow God to maintain ownership of that property during His visible absence? He was not there to enforce His ownership over that property. Would they then come in and steal it, despite the fact that they had been told that it did not belong to them, and that they were absolutely prohibited from touching or eating of that tree?

Satan came to them, and specifically to Eve, and tempted them to violate God's Word. He said that they would not be punished as God had said, that they would not die in the day that they ate of it. All they had to do was to walk over and take a piece of fruit. Nothing to it!

Between the lines, Satan was asking: "Who will notice that anything is gone? God isn't here. The fruit looks good, and there is no reason that men shouldn't have it. God is a monopolist. He is monopolizing control over that tree. Why should God have the right to withhold something important from men? Why was it that He was acting as a tight-fisted individual, pretending that He has the only true control over that property? It's time for man to assert his rights. It's time for man to challenge this monopolistic property owner, God Almighty, who really isn't so mighty after all. Trust me. You'll see that I'm right."

The result, of course, was judgment. Adam and Eve were both brought under the judgment of God, and so was Satan. Mankind's dominion over the earth was made vastly more painful and difficult from that point on. The family was also disrupted, for Cain eventually killed Abel, denying to Abel the private property right to his own life.

Pharaoh, generations later, stole the freedom of the Hebrew slaves (Exodus 1), and stole the land which his own ancestor had delivered to the Hebrews (Genesis 47:5-6). He put them into bondage, just as a kidnapper kidnaps the defenseless. This was to happen again generations later, when the Assyrians took the ten northern tribes, meaning the northern kingdom of Israel, and after that, when the Babylonians captured the southern kingdom: the tribes of Judah and Benjamin. This is a familiar experience in history. Again and again, tyrants have attempted to steal the freedom and the property of their own subjects and of citizens across their borders.

Theft comes in many forms, however. The Bible says, "You shall not steal." The Bible does not say, "You shall not steal, except by majority vote."

Ahab and Naboth

When individuals take advantage of democracy, and vote away the wealth of their fellow men, they are no different in principle from Israel's evil king Ahab, whose reign is discussed in the book, First Kings. In the twenty-first chapter of that book, we have the story of Naboth, an innocent owner of a vineyard. His vineyard was in sight of the palace of the king, and Ahab wanted that vineyard.

When Naboth refused to sell it to the king, because this property was the inheritance of his children, the king was upset. His wife, Jezebel, inquired as to why he was upset, and the king told her. She then hired false accusers who claimed that they had heard Naboth cursing God and the king. So the judges took him outside the city and stoned him to death, as required by Biblical law. Then the king went and confiscated the property of Naboth. (Today, it would be done "in the name of the People.") All nicely legal, you understand.

It was for this that the Lord destroyed Ahab and Jezebel. Ahab had been a corrupt king from the beginning, and he had defied God at almost every opportunity, but it was this sin which led to his downfall (1 Kings 21:17-19).

Socialists, take note. Defenders of the graduated income tax, take note. Defenders of high inheritance taxes, take note. Defenders of redistributing wealth through majority vote, take note. In your lust to confiscate other people's property, you have become false accusers of millions of your fellow citizens, whose only crime is consumer-satisfying productivity.

Self-Interested Voluntary Cooperation

Why is private property so important? There are many reasons. One of the most important is that people become productive because of their motivation to build up their property, to enjoy their property, and transfer it to their children or to those organizations that best represent their goals, ideals, and dreams. Men discipline themselves and serve the marketplace.

Adam Smith, the great economist of the 1770's, argued that it's not to our needs that we appeal when we want the services of the butcher or the baker (unless we are beggars), but to the self-interest of the butcher or the baker in meeting our needs. The *appeal to self-interest*, in fact, is the device—the motivational device—by which we, as individuals, *gain the cooperation* of our fellow man. It's a means, not of control over them, but of rewarding them. It's the way by which we claim attention in the marketplace. We offer them profitable opportunities to serve us and thereby serve themselves.

Would we expect men to labor a lifetime and to sacrifice their present pleasures in order to save for the future, if they expected that at the end of their lives, other men would come in and confiscate their property? Would we expect them to master the difficult skills that are needed in so many professions, if they believed that all of the profits and most of the wages that they earned by the exercise of such skills would be used to support lazy and irresponsible people they have never met? The answer is obvious: *no*! They would no longer make such long-term sacrifices (investments). Society would thereby be deprived of the benefits and blessings of these capital investments.

If God wanted the world to be run in terms of "cooperation by charity," He would never have limited the required tithe to ten percent of one's income. If He wanted "authority by begging," He would never have given men the laws of personal prosperity and cultural economic growth. He wants His people to escape beggary, not build their civilization in terms of it (Deuteronomy 28:1-14).

The Religion of Socialism

The socialist assumes that (1) all property should belong to society, meaning the State; (2) there should be no such thing as private property; and (3) men will work for "society in general" with the same kind of intensity and dedication that they will work for their own families or for themselves. These assumptions are disproved every time they're attempted. That, of course, does not change the mind of the socialist.

The reason why it doesn't change his mind is that *the socialist is a deeply religious person*. He has a very specific view of God, man, and law. He has a very definite opinion of the nature of man. And what he says is that society, through the inauguration of socialistic means of production and socialistic ownership, can transform the very nature of man.

This is basic to the Marxist system, and it's implied in all other socialist systems. It assumes one of two things: (1) man is very different from what the Bible says he is and what we know ourselves to be, or (2) man can be remade by the State to fit the socialist model, the socialist view of the truly dedicated and completely altruistic (selfless) man.

There is another thing to consider. If an individual believes that his property is easily confiscated by the State, his goal will then be to take power over his neighbors by means of politics or bureaucracy. Seeking control over a neighbor's property by means of politics will eventually become much more important to many men than actually producing anything. Thus, not only will economic productivity drop, but people's resources, time, energy, and careful attention will be used to master a means of political theft rather than to actually produce goods and services for consumers.

Does this sound like the twentieth century? It should.

Theft versus Dominion

As theft increases, which is in defiance of the law of God, the ability of society to exercise greater and greater dominion is thereby reduced. People get scared. They start hiding what they own. They start spending money on burglar alarms and locks. Businessmen stop producing as many consumer goods and start producing burglar alarms and locks. Consumers then wind up with more locks and fewer consumer goods. They buy fewer tools. They have to work harder to protect the property that they have, and that amount of property and the value of that property is dropping. Theft reduces honest people's present wealth. More important, it eventually reduces people's economic ability to buy and sell. Theft reduces *future productivity.*

People become more concerned about hanging on to what they have instead of devising new ways to increase what they have by means of lawful dominion. In other words, they are less concerned with serving the needs of the community as a whole, because they have become increasingly paranoid about everyone who comes down the street at night.

As fear grows, people devote more money to crime prevention and theft prevention. This reduces the society's capital base. As capital investment drops, the amount of tools available to workers drops, and the ability of people to subdue the earth productively and fulfill the terms of God's dominion covenant to man (Genesis 1:26-28) also drops. Economic growth is reduced.

Backward Societies

Where can we see proof of this? We see it in the ghettoes of large American cities. We see it in Third World countries. We see it in societies that are dominated by secret societies such as the Mafia. Wherever we find theft becoming a way of life, wherever private property is interfered with, either by the State or private thieves, we find that those societies cannot prosper.

We see evil acts of individuals that increase their personal wealth in the short run. This disturbs us. It certainly disturbed the Psalmist (Psalm 73:3-12). If the civil authorities allow these acts to continue without prosecution, then in the long run, these evil, seemingly profitable acts will reduce the wealth of almost everybody in the society, including even the evildoers.

Where would the average person rather live? In the capitalist West, where there has been a limited amount of theft? Where the State has, until the twentieth century, restrained itself from stealing the wealth of its citizens through heavy taxation? Or would they rather live in some backward agricultural or backward pagan civilization?

Would most people rather be kings in some backward area, or would they rather be middle-class people who enjoy all the benefits of modern medicine, modern technologies, and all the other benefits we have in Western societies? Perverse men who love to exercise power over other people would rather be kings in backward societies, but most people would rather be middle-class citizens in wealthy and growing societies.

Varieties of Theft

There are many forms of theft. It's not just walking into a person's house and taking something. It's not just sticking a weapon in a man's back and demanding that he turn over his wallet.

Fraud is theft. You advertise a product as being of a certain quality, and it isn't. You advertise that your product performs in a certain way, and it doesn't. You tell a person that if he performs a certain amount of work at a certain level, you'll pay him a bonus. But you don't.

It works for employees as well as employers. An individual says he'll work very hard for a particular wage, but he doesn't. A person goes to work on the job, and then spends time talking on the phone to friends, or takes time out of the day to pursue his own affairs. He steals from his employer.

There are many ways to steal from an individual, but all of them involve the same basic impulse. *The thief denies to someone else the right to pursue his own life in his own way.* He denies the other person the right to keep the benefits he earns by his own hard work and risk-taking. The thief hinders the other person in the pursuit of his lawful goals. Theft is stealing the other man's tools and therefore the other man's goals—lawfully pursued goals.

Present-Orientation

This is why theft makes people very present-oriented. They hold on to what they have in the present instead of sacrificing for the future. They decide that the important thing is to enjoy the present while they still have something, before the thieves come and take it away.

This present-orientation is destructive to economic growth. It's destructive of the dominion impulse itself. When people are not willing to sacrifice for the future, work for the future, and plan for the future, their ability to control the future is drastically reduced.

Class and Time

Present-oriented societies are in principle backward societies. Present-oriented societies are lower-class societies. We usually think of a person's class position in terms of how much money he has, but this really isn't accurate. In the long run, a person's position in a particular class is dependent upon his view of the future, and the more present-oriented he is, the lower class he is. He may have a million dollars right now, but if he is a present-oriented individual, he probably will not have the million dollars in a year or two or five. He will have less.

On the other hand, if a person is future-oriented, and he is willing to sacrifice for the future, then it doesn't matter how little he has right now: he will be successful in all likelihood in the future. A graduate student in some skilled profession may not have a lot of money to spend today, but in a capitalist society, in twenty years he probably will have a lot more money to spend than if he hadn't spent the time to get his advanced education. But if you threaten him with extremely high taxation in the future, then why would he sacrifice so much in the present for the sake of his future?

Obviously, he won't. Unfortunately, socialists and those who vote for them refuse to admit the obvious.

The Assault on Civilization

Theft is not simply an assault on an individual. *Theft is an assault on civilization.* It's an assault on the very foundations of civilization. Therefore, one of the most important functions of civil government is to restrict the ability of the thief to tear down society in general. The protection of private property from theft and fraud and violence is at the very heart of civil government.

To the extent that the State in this century has squandered its resources on other kinds of goals besides protection of private property, protection of life and limb, to that extent the State has forfeited its claims to receive support from the public.

When individuals do not honor the law of God by self-government, it becomes extremely expensive for society to protect itself against the loss of its assets. Billions of dollars must be spent in law enforcement, court systems, and all the other devices that defend us against theft. If men were self-governed by the fear of God, and also by their own sense of personal integrity, we would see a drastic reduction in theft and a rapid increase in economic growth and individual wealth.

Restraining Theft

How do you keep a society from indulging in theft? The most important of all restraints is the fear of God. If men believe that God is a perfect Judge, and that He will condemn them through perfect punishment throughout eternity, they will be much more careful about indulging their sins and their lusts. So the first and most important restraint is the *fear of God*. Self-government under God is the primary means of restraint.

Second, it is the responsibility of the family to teach basic principles of righteousness, so the father's role in the early years as a disciplinarian and moral instructor (Deuteronomy 6:6-7) is extremely important.

Third, the preaching of the churches against theft is basic to molding a righteous society. Two thousand years of such preaching made possible the wealth of Western civilization.

Finally, of course, the civil government is the God-ordained earthly agent of punishment. The State is to be an agent of anti-theft, anti-coercion, and anti-fraud.

Theft by Ballot Box

What happens to society if men begin to vote for ownership of their neighbor's property? In other words, what happens if men begin to steal from one another by means of the ballot box? What if they decide to "vote themselves rich" (political covetousness)? More to the point, what if they decide to "vote their richer neighbors poor" (political envy)? What restraint can then be imposed?

If people believe that they can tax other citizens at a higher percentage of taxation than they are burdened with, they will also be tempted to give the State the authorization to confiscate the property of those citizens.

Never forget, the extremely rich members of society always have a sufficient number of lawyers, accountants, and tax loopholes to escape the highest levels of taxation. The people who *at first* are the primary victims of "tax reform" are members of the upper middle class. These are the people who are the most innovative; they are the backbone of Western society. They work smarter than other people (though not necessarily harder). Socialism is designed to break this backbone.

Ultimately, through mass inflation, everyone is pushed up into the highest income tax brackets, and the trap of ballot box theft is sprung on them personally. Surprise, Surprise! God will not be mocked.

One way of restraining people in their lust to get a greater portion of their fellow citizens' wealth is to have all tax rates apply equally to every citizen. This is sometimes called a *flat tax*. In the Bible, it's called the *tithe*. Then, if people vote to increase the rate of taxation, it hurts them as much as it hurts their neighbors.

Socialists and Communists hate the idea of a flat tax. This is why Karl Marx included a highly graduated income tax (higher tax rates for rich people) as the second plank in his ten-part program to destroy capitalism. (*Communist Manifesto*, 1848, last section of Part II.)

The Bible teaches that all laws are to apply equally to all members of society. The Bible teaches that God is not a respecter of persons. This means that God does not play favorites. This is emphasized over and over in the Bible as a principle of justice (Leviticus 19:15; Deuteronomy 1:17; 16:19; Acts 10:34). Laws must not be passed that discriminate against any one segment of the population, unless God's law defines them as criminals.

Conclusion

God's first assignment to man was the assignment to exercise dominion (Genesis 1:28). This is the dominion covenant. This command assumed God's supreme authority over His creation (point one of the covenant). It established a hierarchy: God over man, man over the creation (point two of the covenant). Then He announced boundaries: the forbidden fruit (ethical boundaries: point three of the covenant). Theft was the first crime of man in the garden of Eden. The essence of this crime was a denial of (1) God's supreme authority, (2) His hierarchy of control, and (3) His law.

Men are made in God's image; therefore, when they attempt to steal from other men, they are attacking the image of God. They are in principle repeating the crime of Adam against God. Theft is an assault on the personal integrity and lawful authority of the other individual, and this is indirectly an assault against the integrity and authority of God. Theft is based on a view of the present order of society that says that God has wrongfully or erroneously distributed property. The thief takes things into his own hands—literally. He redistributes property along lines more pleasing to him. He makes himself a little god, a judge of the present social order and the God who established it in history.

Theft interferes with the process of dominion. Men have been assigned the task of exercising their skills and their talents over the earth for the glory of God. This responsibility to take initiative—the dominion covenant—cannot be evaded. It's built into the very nature of man. But it becomes a distorted, evil impulse when men begin to exercise dominion in God-dishonoring ways.

It's imperative that in any society which wishes to follow the requirements of God's plan for man to take dominion over the earth, the authorities in every institution must take measures against theft.

The question then arises: What should the civil government do? We will be covering that question in the second section of this book, but the most important single principle is the principle of *restitution*: restoring goods to their rightful owner. The victims should have restored to them whatever was stolen from them, plus a penalty payment (Exodus 22). This way, the State does not grow larger at the expense of the criminal, nor does the State grow larger at the expense of the victim.

When the State becomes a thief by enforcing a heavy and graduated tax system, or by other coercive laws that interfere with men's voluntary exchanges, then everyone under its jurisdiction becomes a potential victim. When the State becomes a representative thief of a majority of men, nothing is safe again. When the State becomes the agent of corruption, the major institution for the repression of evil doing is thereby corrupted.

If men have larceny in their hearts, and they use the ballot box to make theft legal, then the entire society becomes larcenous, and it will eventually lose its ability to grow and progress. God will not be mocked. Judgment will come upon that society.

The following Biblical economic principles are essential if we are to exercise effective, God-honoring dominion:

1. God is the absolute owner of property.
2. Adam's rebellion was displayed as an act of theft. It began with the desire for something that was not his.
3. Tyranny always involves theft (Pharaoh).
4. The best cooperation is voluntary cooperation.
5. Self-interested people cooperate voluntarily.
6. Beggars don't exercise dominion.
7. Appeals to charity are not to become the primary basis of gaining other people's cooperation.
8. Theft by ballot box is not to become the basis of gaining other people's cooperation.
9. Socialism and Communism are religions of humanism, for they are based on the belief in political man (rather than God) as the supreme ruler.
10. Men's view of time affects their view of life.
11. Present-oriented people suffer from poverty, both of the spirit and the pocketbook.
12. Present-oriented people are lower-class people.
13. Future-oriented people are upper-class people.
14. Christianity is a future-oriented religion.

4

SCARCITY

Then to Adam He said, "Because you have heeded the voice of your wife, and have eaten from the tree of which I commanded you, saying, 'You shall not eat of it': Cursed is the ground for your sake; In toil you shall eat of it All the days of your life. Both thorns and thistles it shall bring forth for you, And you shall eat the herb of the field. In the sweat of your face you shall eat bread Till you return to the ground, for out of it you were taken; for dust you are, And to dust you shall return" (Genesis 3:17-19).

The fourth principle of a Biblical covenant is *the principle of judgment-evaluation*. The covenant specifies penalties for breaking the terms of the covenant. What the economist calls scarcity was God's temporal curse on Adam and Adam's environment. Adam broke God's covenant, so God imposed punishment.

The economist has a technical definition of a scarce resource. If, at *zero price*, there is a greater demand for the resource than supply of the resource, then it's a scarce resource. This means that it's an economic good.

Some goods aren't economic goods. For example, air is not normally an economic good. You don't have to pay for it. But cooled air or filtered air *is* an economic good, and people will pay to get it. They pay the electric company, and they pay air conditioning firms to get it. But if, at zero price, demand is equal to supply, or less than supply, then we are not talking about a scarce economic resource. Simple enough?

Scarcity probably didn't originate as a result of the curse on man. Scarcity became a *burden* on man, however, after the Fall of man in the garden.

An example of something which was scarce prior to the Fall is time. It was not that Adam couldn't live long enough to achieve his goals, but he still had to do *one thing at a time*. To choose to do one thing meant that he couldn't do something else. So he had to allocate (distribute) his time. He had to make decisions about what he was going to do and the order in which he would do it. Therefore, time was never a free (zero price) resource. He would have to give up achieving certain things that he would do in one period of time in order to achieve something else.

Scarcity became a burden, a curse, just as labor became a curse to man. Consider Adam's pre-Fall labor. He worked in the garden. He worked to subdue the earth. Adam named the animals (Genesis 2:19), and he had at least some idea of beauty, for he was to dress and protect the garden (Genesis 2:15). But after the Fall of man, God cursed Adam's labor and man's environment.

The Curse of the Ground

Why did God curse the environment? First of all, as we have seen in Chapter Two, He cursed it in order to show Adam what it was like to suffer disobedience in the lower ranks of the chain of command. God wanted to show Adam what it was like to have the world rebel against him, just as he had rebelled against God.

Another reason for cursing Adam was to remind Adam of the penalties of disobedience. His work would no longer be the completely joyful and fulfilling occupation that it had been before the Fall. The world was now cursed. Weeds and thorns and briars would grow up; they would poke him and stab him. This also was a form of punishment. The world would not be as easy to rule as it would have been had there not been a rebellion against God.

Furthermore, it would take more of his time and effort to subdue the earth. He would have to pay more—give up more benefits and pleasures—in order to achieve his goals in life. In other words, there is no doubt that the curse of the world was a restraining factor on man and a judgment on man.

Benefits

Nevertheless, there were benefits attached to the curse. This is true of all of God's curses. Benefits are to some degree curses, and curses are to some degree benefits. What determines whether a judgment against a certain individual is mostly curse or blessing? Answer: the individual's heart, his goals, and his status before God (saved or lost, covenant-keeper or covenant-breaker) determine whether a judgment is mostly a curse or a blessing.

For example, an individual might inherit a million dollars. He might then quit his job or stop his education, waste the money, and wind up worse off than before he started. The most famous Biblical example of this squandering impulse in the Bible is probably Jesus' parable of the prodigal son. The prodigal son asks for his inheritance in advance before he is mature, before he has earned it, and before he has disciplined himself to be a good steward of that inheritance. His father gives it to him. The young man then goes off to a far city, immerses himself in the sinful pleasures of life, wastes his inheritance, and then finds himself utterly bankrupt during a period of famine and crisis.

He then is forced to make a difficult choice: (1) starve to death; (2) go to work in a pig sty, gathering husks for the pigs (a horrifying choice for a Jew); or (3) throw himself on the mercy of his father, and be restored to the position of a loved son. He unwisely chose the second, and then wisely chooses the third option: *humility* (Luke 15).

This is the plight of every man who sins against God: (1) die now; (2) try to work your way to salvation, and die eternally (hell and the lake of fire) later; or (3) return to God the Father and ask forgiveness. The third choice is the wise one.

But how does the curse of the ground become a blessing to man? The curse of God is clear: the earth now resists man's dominion. This, on the other hand, is a blessing. It's a blessing because we live in a world of sinners and murderers and those who would shed our blood. Cain killed Abel. If men could do anything they wanted without suffering any of the economic consequences of their actions, it would not be safe to walk down any street.

In a world where most goods are scarce, men need the voluntary cooperation of other men in order to achieve their goals. Because the world is cursed with the burden of scarcity, men are pressured to work with one another. Cooperation overcomes scarcity's limits. The kind of cooperation which God requires and blesses is voluntary. It's cooperation under God. It's *moral cooperation*.

Mass Production by and for the Middle Class

Another important aspect in the overcoming of scarcity, obviously, is mass production. We always have had at least some production, but it has been the development of large-scale mass production which has transformed the world. This began as early as the late Middle Ages — from about the year 1000 until about 1500 — and it increased during the period of the Renaissance and the Reformation (1500-1700). The really spectacular increases in productivity, however, began in the 1770's and the 1780's in Britain, and then in the early 1800's in the United States. We call this era the Industrial Revolution.

The secret of the great fortunes was great productivity. In one of the oddest aspects of the market, great personal wealth is normally achieved by creating production systems that combine low prices, high wages, and high profits. Not many people understand this three-fold relationship.

Socialists argue that the rich man becomes rich by taking advantage of other men, those who work for him and those to whom he sells his goods and services. But "wealth by exploitation" is a myth. The way you attract the most efficient and most productive labor is to pay the laborers high wages. ("You get what you pay for!") The way to attract lots of consumers is to offer low prices. The secret of great wealth is to learn how to apply the "secret miracle formula" of free enterprise capitalism: high wages, low prices, and high profits.

This is what Henry Ford did. He found a way to mass produce an automobile, the Model T. In late 1913, he raised wages to the unheard of rate of $5.00 a day. This doesn't sound like much today, but you must understand that this was before mass inflation hit the dollar. Ford paid the highest wages that anyone paid in manufacturing. He also turned out the cheapest cars that anyone had ever seen. In 1915, he introduced a profit-sharing plan for his employees. George Gilder describes what he did:

> In the recession year of 1914, he cut prices twice, and sales surged up while other companies failed. By 1916, he had reduced the price of a Model T to $360 and increased his market share from 10 percent to 40 percent, while the share commanded by General Motors slipped from 23 percent to 8 percent. By 1921, after cutting prices 30 percent during the 1920 economic crisis, Ford commanded a 60 percent share of a market that had grown by a factor of twelve in a decade. By 1927, he had sold 15 million cars, with a sales volume of $7 billion, and the company's net worth, with no new infusions of capital since the original $28,000, had risen to $715 million, including some $600 million in cash. By the same strategy, Ford also dominated the tractor market.[1]

He became a billionaire before he died in 1947. In fact, he became a billionaire by the late 1920's, two decades after he introduced the Model T, and that was back when a billion dollars bought something.

Price Competition

Mass production overcomes scarcity through a particular form of competition. This competition we call price competition. Instead of producing for kings and nobles and the aristocracy, producers begin to produce for the growing middle class. The middle class has vastly more money than all the rich people in the world. Why? Because there are more of them in a capitalist society. You aim at their needs, wants, and desires.

A middle-class consumer, of course, doesn't have much money compared to some prosperous businessman or elite ruler. But if you combine all of the "economic votes"—that is, all of the dollars, or pounds sterling, or marks, or whatever the currency is—of the

---

1. George Gilder, *The Spirit of Enterprise* (New York: Simon & Schuster, 1984), p. 157.

middle-class consumers, they can almost always "out-vote" (out-spend) the rich.

The secret of capitalism is that capitalists have found ways of vastly expanding mass production techniques. The development of interchangeable parts was one of the great inventions of all time, first for weaponry, and then for almost all other products. An important promoter of the use of interchangeable parts was Eli Whitney, who developed these production techniques about the time that he invented the cotton gin, in the 1790's.

Then came the raising of large amounts of capital by the small savings, the nickels and dimes, of poor people. By the development of banks and other techniques for accumulating capital, these nickels and dimes became huge sums of capital. This capital could then be used to find sources of raw materials that had not been discovered before. Better ways of using raw materials, better ways of reducing waste: here was the "secret" of capitalism. It was cost cutting and price cutting above all that made possible the mass production of the modern world.

It was therefore the development of modern capitalism which made possible the vast increase of personal wealth that the Western industrial world has experienced since the 1780's. But this historical development was very much the result of Christianity. Early capitalism was based on a concept of personal self-reliance, the legal protection of private property, voluntary cooperation, open competition, and honest weights and measures (including money). It involved a concept of time which was future-oriented, and a concept of thrift which we now, in looking back, call the Protestant ethic. All of these factors were combined by means of future-oriented, self-sacrificing hard work, and organized people who recognized the value of education. This new worldview based on the importance of education made possible the modern conquest of poverty.

The Socialist Myth of Natural Productivity

One of the most influential of all the myths of socialism is the idea that the world is naturally productive, but existing human laws and institutions unfortunately stifle both the natural productivity

of nature and the natural productivity of man. The socialist concludes that by restructuring the institutions of the world, this in-
nate productivity will flower, and men will work only a few hours
a day in order to achieve all of their economic goals. Their's is a
view, in other words, of a world which really did exist before the
Fall of man, and which they say can be regained simply by the restructuring of legal and economic institutions.

What they propose is a large plan of redistributing wealth by
placing income taxes on the middle and upper classes. (But when
their government spending programs create huge budget deficits,
they rush to impose new sales taxes, which the poor pay.) They
propose that the State become either the *owner* of the means of
production or else the *director* of the means of production. The former system is called Communism or socialism, and the latter system is called fascism or the corporate state. The goal is the same:
an elite body of central planners will, through scientific techniques, plan everyone else's life.

These monopolistic central planners will determine who gets
what, how much, and at what price. By turning the economy into
a single vast hierarchical chain of command, they believe that
they can transform, not simply the nature of man, but the very
nature of nature. Nature will become a land flowing with zero-
price milk and honey.

This is a program of *salvation by law*. It preaches *the regeneration
of society by force*. This program requires *compulsory freedom*. Socialists believe that it will be possible for them to set free "the hidden
forces of productivity" that have been stifled by evil institutions—
primarily the institutions of capitalism and private property.

In short, they don't admit that the world is under God's curse,
that scarcity's burden is the result of man's moral rebellion, and
that productivity is the product of a society's faithfulness to the
covenantal laws of God (Deuteronomy 28:1-14). They don't
believe in salvation by faith in God; they believe in salvation by
man-made laws. They believe therefore in *environmental determinism*.
Change the environment, they argue, and humanity will be
changed. Change the environment by "scientific planning," and

the elite planners can regenerate mankind. They can establish a humanistic New World Order.

The Great Debate: Socialism versus Capitalism

The debate between the socialist and the capitalist is rarely conducted in terms of religious arguments, but in fact the debate is inherently religious. The debate is between rival views of man, rival views of nature, rival views of law, and rival views of God.

The socialist assumes that the Fall of man was not a rebellion against God, but was merely a rebellion against other men which occurred when the first man set boundaries on "his" property and proclaimed himself to be a private owner. The socialist assumes that God did not curse the earth. The socialist assumes that God doesn't require cooperation among men, and at the same time has provided economic incentives for men to cooperate. The socialist relies either on the fear of man (the State) or the altruism of man (self-sacrificing love) in order to achieve mankind's highest economic output and greatest cooperation, one with the other.

The defender of the free market's private property system, on the other hand, acknowledges the depravity and the lusts of man, and the necessity of appealing to men's self-interest in order to create a productive voluntary society. The capitalist doesn't say that all men are by nature good or altruistic. The defender of capitalism says instead that men are self-interested, but that a system of legally protected private property enables society to gain the very best services and the very best efforts from men who otherwise would be selfish, hungry for power, and basically lovers of theft and lovers of destruction.

In short, the free market social order does *not* make men inherently good; only God's regenerating grace can accomplish such a transformation. What the free market social order does is encourage men *to serve the wants and the desires of their fellow man, voluntarily,* because of a unique combination of private property, self-interest, competitive bargaining, and personal responsibility. This incentive system to service is made possible by a legal order which respects the laws of God.

Civil law is not enough. Men also must be self-restrained in their hearts. It's not enough simply to give men the opportunity to work on a free market in search of profit. Larceny is in the hearts of most men. Mankind advances to the extent that mankind disciplines itself. Men must be disciplined—*self-disciplined*.

Law enforcement cannot be directed from a centralized top-down bureaucracy, precisely because there aren't enough economic resources available to watch all men night and day in everything that they do, let alone trying to examine their hearts and motives. All government must be based first on *self-government under law*. Discipline must be imposed on law-breakers by local institutions. Government must be imposed from the bottom up, with a series of appeals courts to judge the evil public actions of men (Exodus 18; Matthew 18). There is no other way to create social order. It would bankrupt society to attempt to achieve the kind of control over men's passions and outward actions that the modern central planner attempts to impose.

Conclusion

Scarcity is a curse of God on man, the ground, and the animals. It was imposed by God because of man's moral rebellion. Man rebelled against God, specifically by stealing what was announced in advance as being "off limits" to man. Men, therefore, were cursed by a special kind of burdensome scarcity by which they would be pressured to labor harder than they would have been forced to labor before the Fall. They were given a scarcity of lifespans, as well, so that they would have to work even harder to achieve their goals. They don't have the same amount of time in front of them that they otherwise would have possessed.

Scarcity is a blessing because it pressures men to cooperate voluntarily with each other. If men are willing to obey the law of God, and to establish those kinds of legal institutions of private and familistic capital that the Bible requires, then it becomes possible for them to overcome many of the limits of scarcity.

Today, Western citizens live in an economic world in which we don't work nearly so hard as our grandfathers did, just as they didn't work nearly so hard as their grandfathers did, and so on, back until the late 1700's. Men don't pour out their lives into the dirt in Western industrial societies. They may get ulcers, and they may suffer diseases, but they live longer. (The judgment of God called AIDS may change this over the next two decades.) They don't have the same problems with sweat that men had from the days of Adam until the twentieth century.

What we find then is that *the curse of scarcity has been increasingly eliminated as men conform themselves ethically to the laws of God and the requirements of God.* All of this can become a snare if men should again forget their Maker and the Giver of the gifts, as we are warned in Deuteronomy 8:17. But the point is, the curse of sweat and the curse of weeds have been progressively eliminated as a result of modern capitalism, which is Biblical law and Biblical economic principles put into action.

Though modern wealth has led to the arrogance of modern man, and may lead to a greater judgment if men refuse to rebuild the kinds of social institutions which created this wealth, we have, nevertheless, been the beneficiaries of a vast outpouring of wealth beyond the wildest dreams of people who lived as recently as the late-nineteenth century. We have been the great beneficiaries of the division of labor, and the result has been a great increase in man's ability to exercise dominion and to rule the world wisely.

If we are to overcome progressively the limitations and burdens of God's curse of scarcity, we need to acknowledge God's principles of wealth. We need to honor these Biblical economic principles:

1. God is the absolute owner of the world.
2. Man rebelled against God.
3. God cursed man and man's environment.
4. Man is required by God to exercise dominion, despite this curse.
5. The curse is progressively overcome by obedience to God.
6. The curse was in part a blessing: it encourages voluntary cooperation.
7. Cooperation is based in large part on personal self-interest.

8. The free market provides incentives for service: the quest for profit.

9. Market competition reduces waste and provides new opportunities for consumers.

10. The most important form of competition under a free market is price competition.

11. The free market increases the size and influence of the middle class.

12. Socialism is based on a false view of man and nature: cooperation and productivity as natural, with private property as the cause of poverty.

13. Socialism teaches salvation by law.

14. The primary form of government is self-government under Biblical law.

5

INHERITING THE WORLD

A good man leaves an inheritance to his children's children, But the wealth of the sinner is stored up for the righteous (Proverbs 13:22).

The fifth and final principle of a Biblical covenant is *the principle of legitimacy-inheritance*. It could also be called the principle of *continuity*. In the field of economics, the principle of inheritance governs the transfer of wealth from parents to children. But the Biblical model of this family transfer is the transfer of property from God to His people.

Adam and Eve were given the garden of Eden to subdue and guard (Genesis 2). They were to use this experience as a training period; from the garden, they were to go out and subdue the whole world. Note: *possession was not automatic*. They had been given the whole world as their lawful legacy from God, but they could not possess it free of charge. They had to earn it, just as children are supposed to demonstrate their ability to manage money before taking possession of the family inheritance.

The First-Born Son

Adam was the first-born earthly son of God, made in his Father's image (Genesis 1:26-27). The New Testament records the family line of Jesus, and ends with Adam, who was "the son of God" (Luke 3:38). The words "son of" were inserted by the translators of the King James edition, but this really was the meaning of the Greek. In tracing Jesus' lineage, the Greek reads: "Joseph, which was [the son] of Heli, which was [the son] of Matthat . . . ," all the way back to Adam. The use of the word "of" implies father-hood. Adam was the son of God.

Adam lost his sonship by rebelling against his Father. He became a *disinherited son*. From that point on, the only way to full sonship before God was by *adoption*. God chooses people to enter into His covenanted family, restoring them by His grace (Ephesians 2:8-9). This is why the Gospel of John announces in the first chapter, concerning Jesus Christ: "But as many as received Him, to them He gave the right to become children of God, to those who believe in His name" (John 1:12).

When Adam placed himself morally under the rule of Satan, he thereby gave Satan an opportunity to steal Adam's original inheritance. Adam was now legally dead in God's eyes. He had given up his inheritance. Satan immediately took possession of the world *as a squatter possesses*, meaning until the lawful heir returns to claim his stolen inheritance.

Through grace, God adopted the Hebrews as His people, and gave them the land of Canaan as their inheritance. In this small bit of real estate in the Middle East, God established His temporary earthly headquarters for the reconquest of the earth.

Jesus Is the Lawful Heir

Jesus Christ is the second-born earthly Son, but the first-born eternal Son, who was with God the Father from the beginning (John 1:1-5). Paul called Him the "last Adam," in contrast to the first Adam (1 Corinthians 15:45). It is He who rightfully inherited what would have been Adam's legacy. Through His perfect obedience to the law of God, He proved Himself to be the lawful heir of the Father.

He announced this in His parable of the absentee landlord. It assumes the original ownership of the world by God. "There was a certain landowner who planted a vineyard and set a hedge around it, dug a winepress in it and built a tower. And he leased it to vine-dressers and went into a far country. Now when vintage-time drew near, he sent his servants to the vinedressers, that they might receive its fruit" (Matthew 21:33-34). Clearly, God owns the field because He created it. He even stocked it with capital assets.

"And the vinedressers took his servants, beat one, killed one, and stoned another. Again he sent other servants, more than the first, and they did likewise to them" (Matthew 21:35-36). The husbandmen were thieves. They wanted the fruits of the field. They were dividing up the land and its fruits "in the name of the People." No more would the distant landlord take advantage of them!

"Then last of all he sent his son to them, saying, 'They will respect my son.' But when the vinedressers saw the son, they said among themselves, 'This is the heir. Come, let us kill him, and seize his inheritance.' And they caught him, and cast him out of the vineyard, and killed him" (Matthew 21:37-39). The husbandmen imitated God, Who had cast Adam out of the garden. The Jews later fulfilled His parable when they dragged Him from the garden of Gethsemane into a "kangaroo court," tried Him, and then had Him executed by the Roman authorities.

What was the point of the parable? That the Jews had slain the prophets, and would slay Him, too. Judgment would come soon thereafter. "Therefore I say to you, the kingdom of God will be taken from you and given to a nation bearing the fruits of it" (Matthew 21:43). In short, they had *given up their inheritance*. They had imitated Adam, rebelled, and would be scattered. They had taken property from its rightful owner, and God promised to take away what would have been theirs.

The implication was world-transforming: *Christ's people have inherited the kingdom*. This kingdom is the whole world.

Jesus and the Jubilee Year

Jesus began His public ministry when He entered the synagogue at Nazareth, and stood up to read the scroll of the Book of Isaiah which had been handed to Him. He read from the section we designate today as Isaiah 61. Jesus read these words: "The Spirit of the Lord is upon Me, Because He has anointed Me to preach the gospel to the poor. He has sent Me to heal the brokenhearted, To preach deliverance to the captives And recovery of sight to the blind, To set at liberty those who are oppressed, To preach the acceptable year of the Lord" (Luke 4:18-19). Then He handed the scroll back to the priest and sat down. He announced to them, "Today this Scripture is fulfilled in your hearing" (4:21).

What had the passage referred to? The jubilee year. What was the jubilee year? Legally and historically, it was an aspect of the military conquest of the land of Canaan. Symbolically, it was an aspect of God's deliverance of His people.

Before the Hebrews captured Canaan, God set up a reward system for the participants in this military invasion. He set up what the politicians call a spoils system. The families that participated in the war would inherit specific pieces of land, tribe by tribe. The future division was outlined by Moses before they came into the land (Numbers 34-36). The only tribe which could not inherit permanent land was the priestly tribe, the Levites. They could hold land only in the cities (Numbers 35:2-7). The jubilee affected them differently (Leviticus 25:32-34).

As an incentive to fight, each family was guaranteed permanent ownership. They were not allowed to deprive their future biological heirs of inheritance. Every fifty years, each parcel of land had to be returned to the lawful bloodline heir of the original family. This was supposed to take place in the famous jubilee year, which is described in Leviticus 25. (There is no historic or Biblical evidence that the jubilee year was ever celebrated.)

The jubilee year followed the seventh sabbatical year in a series: the fiftieth year. Every seventh (sabbatical) year, all debts were cancelled for Hebrew debtors, all Hebrew slaves were set free, and the land rested—no planting or harvesting was done (Leviticus 25:1-7). The seven sabbatical cycles pointed to the coming year of complete deliverance, when the family's land was returned to the lawful heir from anyone who had temporarily leased it. Families that had lost their land were given hope.

In short, the jubilee year was *the year which restored the family's lost inheritance*. It symbolized *the year of full deliverance*. It symbolized *the restoration of all things*.

Christians as the Heirs

God had transferred title to the land of Canaan when He promised Abraham that his heirs would inherit it (Genesis 15:7). They didn't possess it for four generations, as God predicted (15:16). Possession of the inheritance was not automatic.

The land of conquered Canaan was supposed to serve the Hebrews as the garden was to have served Adam: as a training ground. They were to use it as a base of operations in a world-wide program of conquest — *conquest by ethics*. Jonah's ministry was the great Old Testament example. But the Hebrews failed in this task of world-wide evangelism. Satan remained the squatter-inheritor of the world.

When Jesus announced the beginning of His public ministry by proclaiming the fulfillment of the jubilee year, He was thereby announcing the transfer of title: *from the deceased Adam to God's incarnate Son.* What was listed on that deed? *The whole world.* Jesus was claiming His inheritance as God's legitimate son. Satan the squatter was put on notice: the heir has come.

Jesus went out and fulfilled the terms of Isaiah 61: He comforted the brokenhearted, healed the sick, and set spiritual captives free. Then He died on the cross.

The Old Testament laws of inheritance named the *brothers* of the deceased as the lawful heirs, if he left behind neither a wife nor children (Numbers 27:9). Who are Jesus' lawful heirs? His ethical followers. "And He stretched out His hand toward His disciples and said, 'Here are My mother and My brothers!'" (Matthew 12:49). Those who *obey the moral laws* of Jesus are the heirs of His inheritance.

This means that *Christians have legally inherited the world.* This is why Jesus commanded His followers to go out and *disciple* (discipline and rule) the nations (Matthew 28:18). *They are to claim their inheritance in His name.*

The basis today for Christians' collecting their lawful inheritance is hard work, moral faithfulness to God and man, and building up their families' savings. They are to earn their inheritance in the same way that Adam was supposed to earn it: by managing their inheritance wisely—by exercising dominion. They must prove themselves faithful sons.

The jubilee year was fulfilled by Christ, as He announced. Israel's 50-year land-holding cycle is abolished forever, just as the slaying of animals in the Temple is abolished forever. Jesus fulfilled the terms of the jubilee year. The Jews' inheritance in Palestine was taken from them. There is no more need for the jubilee year as a means of repossessing land, for there is no more inheritance based on the original military conquest of Canaan. We have a better jubilee today: *world dominion*. We hold title to the whole world; now we need to fulfill the terms of the dominion assignment in order to prove ourselves faithful sons.

Responsible Sonship

The system of inheritance in the Old Testament was based on a fundamental principle: the *rightful* heir is the *responsible heir*. Normally, the first-born son inherited a double portion (Deuteronomy 21:17). That is, the inheritance would be divided up in terms of its value among the sons, with an added unit. If a man had six sons, the inheritance would be divided into seven parts, with the eldest son inheriting two units.

Why a double portion? Because the eldest son would have the greatest responsibility for the support of the parents. Why not give the daughters an inheritance? They *did* receive the inheritance, if there were no surviving sons (Numbers 27:1-11). If there were sons, they didn't inherit. Why not? Because they were to be given a dowry of money and goods at the time of marriage. Their husbands were responsible for the support of a different set of parents. Presumably, if a son-in-law agreed to contribute to the support of her parents, then he could become a legitimate heir.

Consider what this meant for the first-born son. He would be required to take care of his parents in their old age. He was therefore entitled to the double portion. The parents understood that they could not live forever. They understood that they were under the curse of God because of the sin of Adam. They therefore had to make preparations with respect to the building up of their sav-

ings, and to see to it that in their old age their children would have
sufficient capital to support them. The children, on the other
hand, understood this responsibility, and they looked forward to
inheriting whatever was left over after their parents had died.

Two-Way Responsibility

This system of inheritance involved two-way responsibility.
The first-born son knew that he would be the one most responsible
for the parents, and he also knew that he would inherit a double
portion. The other children accepted the fact that they would not
inherit as much as the firstborn son, but on the other hand, they
didn't have equal responsibility for the care of the parents. In short,
to whom much is given, from him much will be required (Luke 12:48).

The parents had to look to the future in order to build up a
capital base for their children. The children had to be careful to
maintain that capital base, so that they would not have to dip into
their own resources in order to support the parents in old age.
Both generations realized that they had mutual responsibilities to
each other. The father-son relationship or the parent-child relationship was not simply an emotional relationship; it was also covenantal, legal, and economic.

For both parent and child, the family's capital meant a long-
term, future-oriented set of responsibilities. Parents understood
that one of their goals on earth was to pass down a godly inheritance to the children, but since they knew that their children would
be responsible for them in their old age, they also had to pass
down a knowledge of God's laws and understanding of God's ownership. The Proverbs announced that it's the responsibility of
parents to train up a child in the way that he should go, so that in
his old age, the child will not abandon his responsibilities (Proverbs 22:6).

God warned parents to teach their children the law of God:
"And these words which I command you today shall be in your
heart; you shall teach them diligently to your children, and shall
talk of them when you sit in your house, when you walk by the
way, when you lie down, and when you rise up" (Deuteronomy

6:6-7). Faithful parents recognized that they had an obligation both to themselves and to the community at large that their children would be instructed in the Word of God.

Faithfulness to God's law was the basis of inheritance in Israel. It was the realization that parents owed the children a godly inheritance, and that children owed the parents a safe retirement. Thus, there was no large generation gap, because *the basis of mutual service was the Word of God.* Each group could expect payment from the other. At the same time, each group understood its obligations to the other. It was a demonstration of the Biblical principle that *success comes through service* (Mark 9:35), and that capital comes through long-term *efficient* faithfulness (Matthew 25:14-30).

Inheritance Taxes

One of the most disastrous developments of the twentieth century is the almost universal acceptance of the moral acceptability and political necessity of very high inheritance taxes on the rich. This outlook is primarily the result of envy: the hatred of those who are better off, and the willingness to tear them down, even if it hurts those who do the tearing.

Voters know that there are very few rich people. They know that when they vote for politicians who in turn make laws allowing the State to seize rightful inheritance in the form of taxes, there will not be enough confiscated wealth to benefit voters. There simply aren't enough rich people in the world. Even if all inheritances of wealthy people were transferred to the civil government, the amount of money would be so small in comparison with the taxes taken from middle-class people, that no one would even notice the money. The Grace Commission estimated that if all personal income above $75,000 a year in the United States were collected as taxes, this extra revenue would operate the Federal government for only ten days. (And the next year, rich people would hide their income or stop working and taking risks to earn it.)

So who actually gets the rich man's inheritance? Two groups. First, in the private sector in twentieth-century America, it has been the faceless bureaucrats who run the multi-million-dollar foundations that rich men set up in order to beat the tax collectors. Second, in the civil government, it has been the equally faceless Civil Service-protected bureaucrats who run the multi-billion dollar government programs. *Socialism always benefits government bureaucrats* and the politicians who vote for the spending programs.

In short, the demand for high inheritance taxes has almost nothing to do with the actual amount of taxes collected by the government. It has everything to do with envy: *pulling down the successful for the sheer joy of destruction.* The inheritance tax is envy-based, and those who vote for it are envious.

The political popularity of extremely high inheritance taxes on the rich has been universal throughout Western civilization over the last hundred years. The justification for high inheritance taxes is that the children of the rich have done nothing to earn the money. Politicians argue that the parent may have been productive in some venture, or lucky in some venture, but this has nothing to do with the merit of the children.

Short-Run Thinking

The economic error in such reasoning is that it is extremely short run in perspective. One of the motivations of future-oriented businessmen is to lay up a large amount of capital to be distributed among his children. The idea is to pass the skills of capital development on to the children, so that they, too, can continue to expand their dominion over whatever they have been entrusted with by the parents. The idea is to expand the dominion of the family by means of a constantly increasing capital base.

Parents understand that if the sons or daughters don't learn the skills of wise management, these children will eventually lose the money. A wise parent trains his children in the administration of money, service to the community, making a profit in a competitive market, and building up the capital base. If the parent fails to do this, it's obvious that the family's capital base will not survive the second generation, or at least not the third. (The only truly rich family in the United States that has continually expanded its capital for as long as 150 years is the DuPont family.)

The important point is this: the parent has an economic incentive to make good administrators and good businessmen out of his children. If he believes that the State will intervene and take away the money, he has far less incentive to teach his children the skills of business. If anything, he will teach his children the skills of politics.

An Illegitimate Heir

What the State is actually saying when it legislates inheritance taxes is that *the State is in principle the legitimate heir of all families*. The politicians are saying that modern sons and daughters of the rich don't have the right to inherit, since they aren't the ones who will be the ultimate supporters of the parents, meaning "parents in general." Why should "parents in general" object if the State, as their future benefactor and supporter, should inherit the family fortune?

The modern socialist State promises to take care of everybody, if necessary, womb to tomb. For example, the idea is being abandoned which insists that parents are responsible for the education and support of their children. State officials assert that they are responsible for the education and welfare of the children.

Why should children object when the State inherits? After all, the true parent is the State. The State educated them, protected them, and now promises to guarantee lifetime employment to them. (Lifetime employment is the law of the land in the United States: the Full Employment Act of 1946. It says that the government has a legal responsibility for creating conditions of full employment, meaning mass inflation, if necessary.)

Since the State claims authority over the children, this tends to make the parents much more short run in their perspective. They realize that they are not the ones who have the primary responsibility for the education and training of the children. They realize that they have transferred responsibility to another agent, the State. The State understands this also, and politicians assert the new doctrine: *inheritance passes to the State*.

The State promises that the parents will retire on Social Security welfare payments, or other State-managed (ha!) capital.

The children have done nothing to merit the inheritance from the parents, nor are they expected to do anything in the future. *The State first becomes a substitute parent for the children, and it becomes a substitute child for the parent.* The State takes on the responsibility of supporting both the young and the old, so the State naturally demands payment, just as if it were the lawful heir.

There is no escape from the Biblical principle: that *the double portion of inheritance belongs to the son who will take full responsibility for the care of the parents.* The modern welfare State is not only demanding a double portion, but in some cases triple, quadruple, or more.

What we are seeing is *an illegitimate substitution of the State into the role of both parent and heir.* The State has become the bastard pretender. The result is the dramatic expansion of State power over the lives of individuals, and a dramatic increase of State interference into the lives of families.

For those who accept the modern theology of the State as Savior, there is no escape from this kind of interference. It's inevitable, given the initial premise: namely, that the State rather than the family is economically responsible for providing the basic welfare services for members of the family. *Where there is God-honoring responsibility, there will inevitably be authority.* Where there is payment, there will inevitably be requirements. Where there is illegitimately asserted responsibility, there will be illegitimate power.

We don't get something for nothing, whether we ask the State to support us in our education, to support our children in their education, or to support us in our old age. To the extent that we bring the State in as a substitute parent, we automatically bring the State in as a substitute child. The State will capture the inheritance of the ungodly, those who do not obey God's law concerning family responsibility. Why the ungodly? Because when the godly do not fulfill their responsibility, they have become ungodly, and the State will eventually get their inheritance.

The Biblical Response to the Welfare State

The modern State promises to support its citizens from womb to tomb. It educates the children, cares for the aged, and steadily transfers power to the government officials by taking on new responsibilities. It taxes our labor, it taxes our profits, and it taxes our children's inheritance. It has become a substitute parent for young children, and it has become a substitute child for aged parents. It has taken over the economic responsibilities that each generation is supposed to bear. It therefore insists that it is the lawful heir.

In fact, the modern "Savior State" is a bastard pretender. It is one more example of Satan's efforts to maintain control of the inheritance he extracted from Adam. He still keeps control by luring men into sin. In this case, it is the sin of family irresponsibility. It is also the sin of worshipping the State.

How should Christians attempt to recapture the power and authority that the State has taken away? The starting point has to be that parents and family members reassert their responsible role as God's designated institutional source of their own social welfare. *The family is the primary agency of social welfare in every civilization.* State officials may deny this, and they may attempt to transfer to themselves the authority for welfare that the family rightfully holds, but there is no way that the State can completely enforce this transfer of responsibility. Nevertheless, it may go bankrupt trying. It may drive its citizens into bankruptcy, too. The State always extracts wealth from the family in this unjust attempt to become the rightful heir.

"Charity begins at home." This is a famous phrase in American life. It is an accurate phrase. This is *precisely* where charity *must* begin. This doesn't mean that charity is limited only to the home. On the contrary, charity only *begins* at home; it isn't supposed to end there (2 Corinthians 8).

Children must learn the basics of charity, and charity must flow from one home to other households. It's the family which is the primary agency of welfare, and in a community where strong families exist, there will be less and less politically perceived necessity for immoral forms of State-administered welfare.

The only way to achieve decentralized power—capturing power away from the modern socialist State—is to make certain that the family once again becomes the primary agency of welfare. The welfare State is illegitimate. The *welfare family* is the Biblical basis of most social welfare activity. It is the responsibility of the head of each household to care for those members of his family who are in need.

We can see the drift of twentieth-century socialist societies. The State intends to seize the wealth of the just. The State is acting as the political agent of the envious, the incompetent, and the misled. The State is asserting its power over the lives of individuals because it asserts the kind of welfare authority which once was strictly limited to the family. Until families recapture control over the wealth of the family, and lay up capital for godly children and grandchildren to inherit, the socialist State will continue to extract the wealth of the population and waste it. The State will continue to attempt to make itself the only lawful inheritor.

The Biblical solution to poverty and the welfare State is the establishment of private, voluntary welfare programs such as those described in George Grant's Biblical Blueprint Series book, *In the Shadow of Plenty.* Any other solution leads to tyranny. It leads to the creation of a perverse substitute family—one which destroys the capital of those who are "adopted" by it.

Conclusion

Adam forfeited his lawful inheritance when he rebelled against God. Satan claimed this inheritance as an illegal squatter. He conquered the world in one day by Adam's default.

Jesus' ministry restored the inheritance to His people. He announced a world-wide ministry of conquest, based on the preaching of the gospel of peace. Christians are required to pursue the same program of world dominion which God originally assigned to Adam, and reassigned to Noah (Genesis 9:1-17).

There must be continuity over time. Capital must be allowed to grow through time. The basis of this continuity of economic growth over history is inheritance. Capital is transferred down through the generations. The modern welfare State is a satanic attempt to seize the capital of modern man, just as Satan seized Adam's inheritance. It is Satan's last-gasp effort to trick Christians out of their lawful inheritance. To the degree that they adopt his evil theory of the State as welfare agent and therefore lawful heir, God's program of world-wide dominion is delayed.

The Biblical principles of inheritance must be obeyed if Christians are to exercise their dominion responsibilities. They must acknowledge that:

1. God is the absolute owner of all things.
2. He deeded this inheritance to Adam.
3. Adam's moral rebellion led to his disinheritance.
4. Jesus, as the true Son of God, inherited the kingdom of God—the whole world.
5. His death passed His inheritance to His ethical brethren.
6. Adoption comes with God's saving grace.
7. Adopted children inherit God's kingdom.
8. This lawful title to the world is to be collected by Christians.
9. The basis of collecting the inheritance is godly labor, thrift, and leaving an inheritance.
10. The welfare State is demonic.
11. Inheritance taxes are demonic.
12. The family is the primary agency of welfare.
13. Charity begins at home, and spreads out.
14. Where there is responsible behavior, authority follows.
15. Christ completely fulfilled the jubilee year.
16. Land tenure is no longer governed by the provisions of the jubilee year.
17. Immoral children must be disinherited before the parents die.
18. The most competent and morally faithful child should inherit a double portion.

6

"NO TRESPASSING!"

> You shall not remove your neighbor's landmark, which the men of old have set, in your inheritance which you will inherit in the land that the Lord your God is giving you to possess (Deuteronomy 19:14).

In the second half of this section of the book, I intend to provide examples of how men are legitimate rulers under God, and why the same five-point covenantal pattern reappears in the affairs of men.

The first principle of a Biblical covenant is transcendence. God is the Creator. How does this apply to man in his relation to the creation? Man is made in God's image. Therefore, man is a ruler over creation, too.

In the Old Testament, the guardians of God's holy sanctuary were the priests. This is why the Old Testament occasionally refers to the religious leaders as gods. "God stands in the congregation of the mighty; He judges among the gods. How long will you judge unjustly, And show partiality to the wicked?" (Psalm 82:1-2). Men are rulers, or judges, over the creation. "I said, You are gods, And all of you are children of the Most High. But you shall die like men, And fall like one of the princes" (Psalm 82:6-7). God's judgment was to fall on the religious leaders just as it was about to fall on princes. They all judged unrighteously.

Thus, men are to exercise their rulership over the creation, which is similar to the absolute rulership which God exercises over His creation. This is what the first principle of the covenant, the Creator-creature distinction between a transcendent God and

74

dependent men points to. Man is God's image and God's lawful representative on earth.

The Landmark

The landmark is what established the boundary lines of a particular family's property. We use a similar technique today: surveying. When we apply this Biblical law today, we make it illegal to tamper with court records that identify particular plots and their owners. We even have title insurance, so that if some irregularity in the history of the ownership of the property is discovered, and someone else can prove that he owns it, the initial buyer is paid for his loss by the insurance company.

The person who owns a piece of land has the right to exclude most people most of the time. There are a few exceptions to this rule. In emergencies, the police, as officers of the court who have been issued court orders or warrants, have the legal right to intrude on otherwise protected private property. But the owner has the legal right to keep people from coming onto his property most of the time.

The fence is a sign of this right, or the locked gate. The locked door on a home is another example. The idea is that "a man's home is his castle"—a legal fortress which must be respected.

When some property owner sticks a "No Trespassing" sign at his gate, or somewhere inside the boundaries of his property, his wishes are legally enforceable. He has the legal right to keep people off his property. *The legal right to exclude someone from using your property is the essence of all ownership.*

There are limits on this right of exclusion. For example, Biblical law says that a traveller who walks along the highway has the right to pick food from privately owned farms. He does not have the right to place the food in baskets or in the folds of his garment, but he has the right to whatever he can carry away (Deuteronomy 23:25). Jesus and His disciples picked corn on the sabbath, but the Pharisees didn't criticize them for stealing, only for taking corn and rubbing it together on the sabbath (Luke 6:1-5).

Nevertheless, there are only a few cases of such exceptions to exclusion. Property ownership is supposed to be widely dispersed in a Bible-based society, and this means that many people are to have near-exclusive use of their property.

Obviously, the principle of boundaries and the right of exclusion applies to other forms of property besides land. Therefore, we need to consider the concept of the boundary.

The Original Boundary

God set Adam and Eve in the garden. "Then the Lord God took the man and put him in the garden of Eden to tend and keep it" (Genesis 2:15). What does "to keep" mean? It means *to keep something away from someone else*. To keep the garden away from whom? From the intruder, Satan. They were to maintain it under God's authority as His appointed agents.

This means that they were required to put a kind of "No Trespassing" sign inside the garden against all those who would challenge the law of God. Satan then came to them and tempted them to disobey God, to accept the devil's interpretation of the law rather than God's.

What was the law's requirement? That they respect the boundary God had placed around the tree of the knowledge of good and evil. It was "off limits" to them. They could not touch it (Genesis 3:3) or eat it. It didn't belong to them.

God had excluded them. This pointed to His position as the original and ultimate owner of the property. It reminded them that they were under God's rule. They were His subordinates. But it also served to remind them of their responsibilities as keepers of the garden. They, too, were to serve as guardians. They were to keep out any intruder. Because God, as supreme and absolute owner, could legally keep them away from His property, so were they given power by God's law to keep Satan away from their property (meaning God's property which He had entrusted to them).

The moment that they stole God's property by invading the forbidden boundary, they had in principle abandoned the garden, as well as the world outside, to the devil. If they could rightfully assert their power by violating God's property, then Satan could rightfully violate their property, too. If they were not willing to honor another Owner's right to exclude them, to what law could they appeal to enforce their property rights? They had violated the rights of the cosmic Enforcer. Who could then enforce their claims against Satan?

By accepting the legitimacy of theft, they became the victims of the greatest thief in the universe. By accepting this cosmic thief's interpretation of God's property rights, they thereby placed themselves under Satan's moral (immoral) rule. They acknowledged their belief in his view of Biblical law. What could they say against him after their act of rebellion?

Exclusion: Property

God then came to judge them all. He threw them all out of the garden: Adam, Eve, and Satan. Humans would no longer be given physical access to the tree of life, the source of eternal life (Genesis 3:22-24). He placed angelic beings and a flaming sword at the entrance in order to keep them out. His property's boundary was marked by a "No Trespassing" sign of real power. He would no longer rely on their self-discipline to keep them away from His property. He imposed immediate punishment.

God didn't abolish private property when He cursed Adam and Eve. On the contrary, he reinforced it. The garden itself testified to the legitimacy of "No Trespassing" signs. Before their rebellion, the tree of the knowledge of good and evil had been temporarily prohibited. Now the entire garden became permanently prohibited. God did not abandon the principle of "No Trespassing"; He actually reinforced it by placing angelic guards and a flaming sword as restraining factors.

Thus, men still retain the right to exclude others from their property. They too can call upon the civil government to impose physical or other sanctions against those who violate their exclusive ownership, just as God called upon His angels to enforce His exclusive ownership.

Dominion relies on exclusion. Individuals are placed in authority over property, and they are held legally accountable by God for the administration of this property. If they misuse their property (for example, if they use it as a weapon) and violate other people's use of their property, then they are held legally accountable by the civil government and by church government if they are church members.

Not only are they legally accountable, but they are also economically accountable. As I have argued earlier, they are held economically accountable by consumers. If they refuse (or are unable) to use their property in an efficient (low-waste) manner to meet market demand, they suffer losses. Ownership is a social function.

The first time that civil authorities allow thieves to have their way in the community because the State refuses to punish them, or refuses to require convicted criminals to repay their victim (Exodus 22), the State has begun to weaken the defense of property. If citizens encourage their political representatives to vote away the property of others, they themselves have become partners in the crime. Socialism and other kinds of political wealth redistribution are forms of theft. Why? Because the State is violating the right of present property owners to legally exclude other people from the use of their property or the fruits of their labor and property. The State begins to exclude rightful owners from their own property. Exclusion is inescapable. The question is: Who will exclude whom, and on what basis? Will power rule, or will God's law? Will God's law determine who should be excluded, or man's law?

Redeemed men are to increase their authority and dominion. They are to progressively exclude Satan's followers from positions of authority, in every area of life. How is this to be done? Not by the exercise of power, but by the exercise of following God's law. Redeemed men are to compete. They are to get rich through productivity. They are to give money away, in a grand exercise of charity. They are to run for political office, especially at the local level, where the Bible says that primary civil responsibility is to be located. They are to bear more and more responsibility in every area of life. *Power flows to those who bear responsibility.*

In short, *the exclusion of the unrighteous from positions of public power* is to be accomplished through the enforcement of Biblical law. First and foremost, by the Christian's self-government under Biblical law. Second, by Christians gaining majority political support among the voters in favor of Biblical law. Third, by enforcing Biblical law publicly. This means the steady and systematic replacement of today's humanist judges with judges who agree to enforce Biblical law.

Let us make no mistake: Christian dominion necessarily involves the exclusion of anti-Christians from positions of public power. This is in part a political process. It is a bottom-up process, not a top-down process. But there must be winners and losers politically. Our goal as Christians is to make political and cultural losers out of the humanists and satanists. We must do this through better performance, better organization, and the blessings of God. God's elect must win the elections.

Exclusion: Marriage

The eighth commandment is very clear: "You shall not commit adultery" (Exodus 20:14). The tenth commandment is also very clear: no man is to covet another man's wife (Exodus 20:17). (This law also applies to wives who covet other women's husbands.) The sanctity of marriage is to be preserved by all of God's covenantal authorities: church, State, and family. All three institutions are to impose punishments (sanctions) against those who violate marriage by committing adultery.

This is very clearly a case of the right of exclusion. It is a lifetime "No Trespassing" sign at the bedroom door. Most people who favor a mild form of socialism—the so-called welfare State—would probably admit that the exclusionary aspect of marriage is not the same as the exclusionary aspect of private property. They would say that the right to exclude others is legitimate when it comes to personal relationships, but not with respect to economic goods.

Yet it is interesting to note that as the philosophy of the welfare State has become widespread, divorce and adultery have also become commonplace. Is this merely a coincidence?

Inherit the Earth

Marxian Communism

In 1848, Karl Marx and Frederick Engels published the famous *Communist Manifesto*. In Part II of that book, they freely admit: "In one word, you reproach us with intending to do away with your property. Precisely so; that is just what we intend." On the next page (of my English-language edition) they go on to call for the abolition of the family. They are careful not to call for this openly (they were writing a popular tract), but they say that "bourgeois marriage," meaning one man-one wife, is in fact corrupt because there is adultery in society. Therefore, Communism only has to admit what is already supposedly the case: "a system of wives in common." They say: "The Communists have no need to introduce the community of women; it has existed from almost time immemorial." This is nonsense historically; it makes a weak excuse for this evil aspect of Communism.

Engels himself later made this remarkable observation: "It is a curious fact that in every large revolutionary movement the question of 'free love' comes to the foreground." Of course it does: *what the revolutionaries hate is Christianity's principle of legal exclusion.* What they hate is God's right to exclude them from eternal life, and every aspect of exclusive legal rights points to the legal right of God's people to enjoy God's favor on earth and in eternity.

It should not be surprising to learn that Engels never married and had several mistresses, and that Marx seduced his wife's lifetime maid (yes, "Dr. Communism" had a full-time, lifetime servant) and was the father of her illegitimate son, Fred Demuth.[1]

During the first two decades of Communism in the Soviet Union, there was free love, widespread abortion, and easy divorce. Then, in the mid-1930's, Stalin saw what was happening to the family. Birth rates dropped, production sagged, and Communist society was beginning to disintegrate. He reversed the earlier free love doctrines and drastically strengthened the State's enforcement of family ties. That decision saved the Communist experiment.

---

1. Robert Payne, *Marx* (New York: Simon & Schuster, 1968), pp. 265-67.

In 1965, just a few months after the removal of Nikita Khrushchev, the Soviet Union again reversed itself at the same time that the whole non-Communist Western world also reversed itself, and began to introduce family planning (mainly by cheap State-funded abortions). The Bible speaks of the dog who returns to its vomit (2 Peter 2:22); so also do socialist societies eventually return to anti-family practices. They hate the idea of the right to exclude, in every area of life.

But the concept of exclusion is inescapable. The socialists and humanists want people to exclude babies from life. They want people to "keep their gardens" away from crying infants. Again, it is not a question of exclusion vs. no exclusion. It is always a question of who excludes whom, and on what basis.

Exclusion: Adoption

We have all heard horror stories about how a family adopts an unwanted child, and later on the biological mother changes her mind and decides that she wants "her" child. She goes to court and gets some God-hating judge to award her custody of the child. The police accompany the "mother" and hand the child over to her.

Consider the anguish of the parents. They have invested love on that child. Their emotional commitment is very great. They have thought of themselves as responsible guardians of that child, and yet the biological mother's preferences are honored. She wins back the child, despite the child's protests and the parents' protests. Adoption—God's covenantal solution to the sins of man (John 1:12)—is considered second-rate parenthood by the humanistic judges of a society that faces God's judgment.

To avoid this sort of horror, parents hire lawyers (at high fees) to insure that the original mother cannot do this to them in the future. State-licensed adoption agencies go to great lengths to conceal the name of the biological mother from the adopting parents, and equally great lengths to conceal the name of the adopting parents from the biological mother. Without these legal assurances, adoptions become too risky.

The same is even more true of God's legal adoption of us,

redeemed humanity. He gives us the power to become His sons (John 1:12). Once this adoption takes place, Satan cannot challenge God's legal claim as Father to His people. This is why Paul could write: "Who is he who condemns? It is Christ who died, and furthermore is also risen, who is even at the right hand of God, who also makes intercession for us. Who shall separate us from the love of Christ? Shall tribulation, or distress, or persecution, or famine, or nakedness, or peril, or sword?" (Romans 8:34-35). He then answers his own rhetorical question: "For I am persuaded that neither death nor life, nor angels nor principalities nor powers, nor things present nor things to come, nor height nor depth, nor any other created thing, shall be able to separate us from the love of God which is in Christ Jesus our Lord" (Romans 8:38-39).

God has exclusive claims on the lives of all people. As limited creatures, none of us has an unlimited claim on anything or anyone, for only God has unlimited claims. But we do have legitimate limited claims on each other: as marriage partners (1 Corinthians 7:4-5), as parents (Exodus 20:12; Ephesians 6:1-3), as church members (Ephesians 5:21), and as citizens (Romans 13:1-7).

These claims are defined and described by Biblical law. They are therefore *protected* relationships. We are speaking of legal protections for mutual ownership (exclusion). For example, parents cannot legally beat their children to death, but they can legally impose physical punishment, and the Bible insists that they must. A parent who refuses to do this hates his child (Proverbs 13:24). (Look up the listing of the word "rod" in *Strong's Concordance*, especially in the Book of Proverbs.) So the State has some degree of control, but it is minimal. It can protect a child's life—a legal boundary, or legal exclusion—but not his behind. It cannot legitimately prohibit physical punishment of children by parents or by those who have been given legal power by parents to represent them in giving physical punishment (school teachers).

Socialists hate the idea that God excludes from eternal life all those who hate Him. This division between saved and lost is horrifying to them. They do their best to exclude Christianity and its evil doctrine of God's exclusive eternal favor to some (but not all) men. Wherever socialism is widely believed by the people, the church is persecuted, or at least discriminated against. Socialism is inherently anti-Christian, and Christianity is inherently anti-socialist.

Exclusion and Dominion

The model of adoption is basic to the model of property ownership. If God establishes His eternal claims of ownership over mankind, it should not surprise us that He also holds men responsible for the administration of His property.

The administration of property is a training ground for dominion. This means that certain people must be made legally and economically accountable before God and other men. They need the right to exclude other people from their lawful property if they are to become wise managers of that property. They also need this protection as an encouragement to make the heavy sacrifices necessary to make any project pay off. The sacrifices of owners in increasing their property are similar to the sacrifices of adoptive parents. Adoptive parents insist on (and need) the assurance that their position as parents will be upheld by civil law. So do property owners.

Property ownership is not to become some monopoly of an elite corps of State-appointed or State-elected officials, any more than parenthood is. It is not simply some distant bureaucracy which is to possess the exclusive right of keeping others from "State" property (meaning, ultimately, property controlled by the administrators). Every man is to be encouraged to become a property owner—a responsible steward before God. Decentralized property ownership takes advantage of the Biblical principle of the division of labor.

It is interesting that in communist societies, from Plato's utopian (nowhere) "Republic" to modern Soviet society, State officials have demanded parental rights over children. They set up day care centers and require working mothers to leave their children under State care. Furthermore, compulsory education in State-licensed schools is a universal aspect of the modern Savior State.

Rushdoony was correct when he titled his book on State-financed education *The Messianic Character of American Education* (Craig Press, 1963). The State as Savior is the vision of progressive educators, as Rushdoony proves from their writings. A Bible-honoring Christian identifies compulsory State education as a form of legalized kidnapping.

Conclusion

God excluded Adam and Eve from the tree of the knowledge of good and evil. They, in turn, were to exclude Satan from the garden by pronouncing God's judgment against his lies, and then wait for God to return to the garden to judge him. Adam, Eve, and Satan were then excluded from the garden by God as a punishment. In the case of humanity, this was necessary to exclude them from eternal life on terms other than God's gracious adoption. They were to be kept from the tree of life.

Property is scarce—land, skills, good will, and all other forms of salable wealth. This means simply that at zero price, there is more demand for scarce property than supply. Thus, every society must find ways to exclude certain people from control over specific pieces of property. There is no escape from the concept of exclusion. It is an inescapable concept. The two relevant questions are these: Who will exclude whom, and on what basis?

The Bible says that God excludes the lost at the day of judgment. It also says that the family and the economy are to be based on the right of individuals to own private property and to exclude others from access to their family members and the property of the members. This outrages socialists, who want the State alone to possess this right of exclusion.

The Biblical principle of exclusion leads us to the following conclusions:

1. God, as the sovereign owner, excludes men from whatever He chooses to keep for Himself.
2. He chooses some for eternal life (adoption, John 1:12), and excludes others (Romans 9).

3. He delegates to men a limited legal power to exclude others in every area of life.

4. Redeemed men are to take dominion from Satan's followers in every area of life.

5. Redeemed men are therefore to exclude rebellious men from ownership in every area of life.

6. The means of lawful economic exclusion is productivity within a competitive market, not political force.

7. This power of exclusion operates in every area of life: family, church, State, business, education, etc.

8. Exclusion is basic to dominion: it is the training ground for personal responsibility.

9. Ownership (the right to exclude) of property is not to be violated by the State, just as the right to exclude others in marriage is not to be violated.

10. The State is not to become the single owner; therefore, the State cannot legitimately abolish private property.

11. Socialism is theft: the illegitimate exclusion by the State of lawful owners.

12. Socialism is therefore anti-dominion and pro-power.

13. Socialism is historically and theoretically anti-family.

7

DEBT BONDAGE

The rich rules over the poor, And the borrower is servant to the lender (Proverbs 22:7).

A continuing theme in both the Old Testament and the New Testament is the danger of debt. The Bible is clear: the borrower is servant to the lender. This principle of debt-free living is an aspect of the second principle of a Biblical covenant.

The second principle of a Biblical covenant is the principle of authority-hierarchy. There is no escape from authority and hierarchies: the dominion of some men over others according to their ability. Hierarchy is an inescapable concept. It's never a question of hierarchy vs. no hierarchy. It's only a question of *which* hierarchy. It's a question of who rules over whom in which spheres of life.

In the field of applied economics, the principle of authority applies in several areas: employer-employee, master-servant, teacher-apprentice, and so forth. The Biblical response to God in the field of personal economics is the *tithe*: God is to be honored by a payment of ten percent of our increase after taxes. (God does not expect us to pay Him for any increase which has been eaten by locusts or the modern equivalent of locusts, tax collectors.) We acknowledge our obedience to Him by paying Him His tithe.

Tithing tells God and men just who it is who is our Master. It tells them that we are under God's authority, not just in the future world, but today, on earth. We owe God a tithe, but only after He has given us the increase. He "wins" when we win. We owe Him no payment in the future if we gain no increase. If we only live off

86

of our existing capital, we owe Him no formal payment. In short, "no gain, no pain."

Debt and Subordination

Not so with the indebted person. There may be no future gain, but there will be future pain. The debtor has placed himself under a master. He has sold a portion of his future increase. He has asserted in principle that he will get this increase. He has risked becoming a visible servant because he has contractually boasted concerning his economic future.

The Bible teaches very clearly that man cannot serve two masters. He either serves God or he serves mammon, the god of greed. The meaning is obvious: God is the absolute ruler and owner of all creation, and the only person to whom man should be in debt. When a man borrows money from another individual, he promises to return that asset, and he usually also promises to return additional assets (interest). He therefore has made a vow to that other individual. He has made a promise. If the promise is a legal transaction, as it usually is in debt relationships, he has pledged not only his name and sacred honor to that individual, but he has also pledged his future.

The Old Testament took debt very seriously. Old Testament law allowed an individual and his family to be sold as temporary servants in order to repay a debt (Leviticus 25:39-43). He became the social equivalent of a sojourner, a foreign believer who lived in Israel (Leviticus 25:40)—a humiliating prospect for a Hebrew. If an individual borrowed money or goods from another individual in Israel, that individual to whom the debt was not repaid could compel the authorities to offer the debtor up for purchase. A third party could come in, pay the creditor whatever was owed to him, and take the debtor into bondage.

The Year of Release

There were time limits on how long he could be forced to serve. In Deuteronomy 15, we are given information about this limited period of time that a Hebrew could be put into slavery: "At the end of every seven years you shall grant a release of debts. And this is the form of the release: Every creditor who has lent anything to his neighbor shall release it; he shall not require it of his neighbor or his brother, because it is called the Lord's release" (Deuteronomy 15:1-2). This special year has been called the *sabbatical year*. It came every seven years.

Obviously, as the year of release drew closer, the debtor would draw closer to the time at which, by law, the creditor would have to forfeit whatever was owed to him. For charitable loans, this meant that the creditor could suffer considerable loss. This is why God warned His people: "Beware lest there be a wicked thought in your heart, saying, 'The seventh year, the year of release, is at hand,' and your eye be evil against your poor brother and you give him nothing, and he cry out to the Lord against you, and it become sin among you. You shall surely give to him, and your heart should not be grieved when you give to him, because for this thing the Lord your God will bless you in all your works and in all to which you put your hand" (Deuteronomy 15:9-10).

Understand, we are talking here about the *poor* brother in the Lord. We are talking about a charitable loan. Just because that loan became more and more risky as the year of release approached, God warned that the potential creditor should not close his hand of generosity to the needy brother. If he did, the needy brother could legitimately cry unto the Lord, and the Lord would count it as sin on the part of the creditor. On the other hand, if the creditor did extend the loan to the man, the creditor could then expect the blessing of God in the future.

Usury

There is another aspect of loans for the poor which must be considered. It was illegal in Israel to charge any form of interest to the Hebrew brother who came for a charitable loan. To charge interest on such a loan was called usury (Leviticus 25:35-38). It was lawful to collect the principal sum that had been lent to him, but it was not legal to extract any additional interest payment. "Usury" in the Bible means any increase in the amount of repayment above the principal, *but only in the case of charitable loans.*

Historically, this has been misinterpreted by many churches, especially in Medieval times. It was assumed by church authorities that this prohibition on interest applied to business loans as well as charitable loans. This is not the case. It applied only to charitable loans. Similarly, some churches interpreted high interest as usury. This also is incorrect. Usury is not defined as high interest, but as *any* interest payment on *charitable* loans.

Thus, the lender is giving a subsidy to the borrower. The lender could have kept the money, or invested it in some other line of business, in the hope of achieving a profit. He couldn't do this when he lent the money to a needy Hebrew brother. God served as the source of the interest payment. God promised to reward the individual who was charitable to his brother in the Lord. In other words, God agreed to step in and provide the increase in response to an open hand and an open heart. This pointed to the mercy of God as one of the characteristic features of God. This pointed also to the need of all men to have God step in and make up any loan obligation on their part, since all men are debtors to God.

We see once again that economic relationships are tied very closely to theological and ethical issues. We are debtors to God, and we need someone to help us—not simply to make the next interest payment, but to step in and make the actual payment of the principal to God the Father. This is what Jesus Christ did on Calvary. "For you were bought at a price, therefore glorify God in your body and in your spirit, which are God's" (1 Corinthians 6:20).

For an individual to be merciless to someone in need when he does have the extra assets available to help that person, is, in effect, to deny that he, too, is a debtor to God, and is also in desperate need for God to intervene and repay his own debt. In other words, it's an assertion of autonomy, an assertion of sin-free living, and finally, an assertion that there is no Judge who intervenes in the name of the righteous, and who brings devastation to those who are unrighteous.

Enslaving Unrighteous Debtors

Does this mean that we are to lend to anyone who asks for a loan? No. We must make judgments about the actual conditions of need on the part of the individual who requests the loan. We have to decide whether or not the person has willfully and lawlessly wasted his capital. For example, if we know that the person who asks for the loan is going to go straight to a bar to get himself a drink, and thereby neglect his own family, we don't give that person anything. We may wish to seek out his wife or children in order to help them, but we owe that individual nothing. We do not subsidize evil.

In the Old Testament, when a foreigner came to a Hebrew to ask for a loan, not only could the lender demand an interest payment, but he could also require payment beyond the seventh year of release. Was this unfair? No. What this pointed to was that the individual who refused to follow God's laws was in fact asserting his independence from God, his own sin-free condition, and his faith that there is no final Judge as described in the Bible. Such a person refused to serve God. Therefore, such a person could be dealt with as a *true slave*, for there is only one alternative to service to God: service to the devil. In order to bring the devil's disciples under dominion, it was legal for a Hebrew to make long-term loans to foreigners, and to extract again all of the money or goods owed to him. At least in this way, God would receive a tithe on the increase.

Again, we see theological and ethical themes governing economic relationships. The foreigner was an unbeliever. The foreigner would not commit himself to a personal relationship to God. Therefore, the foreigner was regarded as the enemy of God, and was not entitled to the same economic mercy which God had advised in relationships between believers. Because the foreigner, if he remained an outsider to the covenant of God, was headed for final judgment, God allowed the Hebrew to extract interest payments and payment beyond the seventh year of release. This lack of mercy pointed precisely to the eternal future of that foreigner.

He was reminded that since he would not place himself under the earthly mercy of God, he was not going to be entitled to be placed under the eternal mercy of God. Thus, the debt relationship became a threat to him, because of the principle that the borrower is servant to the lender.

Consider the promise of blessings in Deuteronomy 28. "The Lord will open to you His good treasure, the heavens, to give the rain to your land in its season, and to bless all the work of your hand. You shall lend to many nations, but you shall not borrow" (Deuteronomy 28:12).

Israel was to become the dominant nation of the world, but only for as long as the people of Israel remained faithful to the terms of God's covenant. This meant that Israel would loan money abroad, and would thereby become dominant in foreign lands. This doesn't mean that the state of Israel, meaning the civil government of Israel, was to have become the agency of lending. It probably refers to foreign traders who went out to bring goods and services to foreign lands, and who would lend money in order for the foreigners to purchase the goods, and who would become the dominant influence abroad.

Consider also two of the curses found in Deuteronomy 28: "The alien who is among you shall rise higher and higher above you, and you shall come down lower and lower. He shall lend to you, but you shall not lend to him; he shall be the head, and you shall be the tail" (Deuteronomy 28:43-44). Here again, we see *debt as the instrument of conquest*, and in this case, it's the foreigner who is within the gates who is the superior person in the arrangement. It is he who has the capital assets to lend to the Hebrew. It is he who establishes the terms of the loan, and therefore, it is he who is "in the driver's seat."

Enslaving the Creditors

We look at today's world, and we find that the debtor-servant relationship no longer seems to hold. Today, the West has lent hundreds and hundreds of billions of dollars to bankrupt backward nations that are unable to repay the money. Specifically,

Western banks and Western governments have lent money to finance the schemes of politicians in backward nations. These backward nations now threaten the very banking system of the West. If they should default on the loans overnight, the West's banking system might collapse.

This seems to oppose what the Bible teaches. It seems now that the creditor is servant to the debtor. It's now a disadvantage to be a creditor, and an advantage to be a debtor. Why is the modern world seemingly a refutation of the Biblical principle of debt and servitude?

Modern Mass Inflation

The primary difference is that in the modern world, the State has the power to create money. This was not the case in ancient Israel. Because the State has this monopoly of money creation, debtors seek to capture the power of the government, and then produce large quantities of inflated money, in order to repay the creditors with far less valuable assets. Because money is a monopoly of the State, the control of money becomes a political objective. The control of money through politics therefore has reversed the relationship of power and authority between debtor and creditor: the creditor in an economy based on politically controlled money can become the *political captive* of the debtor.

In the modern world, in almost all cases, the long-term creditor eventually is destroyed by the inflation. The long-term debtor is able to pay off his obligations with worthless money. The classic example of this is Germany in 1923. So rapid was the inflation, 1921-23, that at the end of the inflation in November of 1923, it would have been possible to pay off the entire mortgage indebtedness of pre-war Germany (about 40 billion German marks) with the marks you could have bought in the black market for about a third of an American penny (one dollar = 100 pennies). Had you confined yourself to transactions in the legal currency exchange markets, you could have paid it off with a penny. This was the taking of money that rightfully belonged to creditors on a historical scale never seen before.

In the Old Testament, the State did not control money. The State *protected* money, because it enforced the Biblical law concerning honest weights and measures, but the State did not issue money. Money consisted of gold and silver bars of a particular weight, shape, and fineness. (I have explained this Biblical money system in greater detail in my book in the Biblical Blueprint Series, *Honest Money*.) Thus, when the debtor had to repay your debt in a privately issued but State-defined currency which could not be legally inflated, he was in fact servant to the lender. If the debtor ever wanted another loan, if the debtor ever wanted to escape the humiliation of debt servitude, he had to repay the loan. When the State honors the principle of honest weights and measures, and when the State goes so far as to allow temporary indentured servitude of the debtor in order to repay the creditor, then it is true that the borrower is servant to the lender.

Escape from God

What we see in the modern world is the attempt of the modern humanistic man to escape the law of God. What we see is an attempt on the part of lawless men to reverse the relationship between the creditor and the debtor. Modern man wishes to convert his weakness as a debtor into a position of power over the creditor. In other words, it's an attempt of the man who has fewer assets and greater liabilities to dominate the man with a large number of assets and few, or even zero, liabilities.

Once again, we see reflected in the economy of man an assertion of a particular theological perspective. Modern man does not want to admit that he is a debtor to God. He wishes to pay God off with "depreciated money." What this means is that he expects to work his way into heaven. He expects his worthless rags, as the Bible calls man's attempts to live independently of God (Isaiah 64:6), to be sufficient payment to repay God for the rebellion of Adam in the garden, and the rebellion of every man from the moment of his birth until the day that he dies. The humanistic, God-defying debtor is asserting his own sovereignty and his own power over the creditor. Thus, a *theological rebellion* on the part of man has led to an *economic rebellion* on the part of man.

The Gambler

The gambler believes in the run of luck which may last only an evening or at most a few weeks. He knows that no run of luck goes on forever, so he is willing to risk everything on the turn of a card or the roll of a pair of dice. If he thinks his run of luck has begun he will sacrifice everything in order to continue to expand his capital base in a very short run operation.

Consider also the psychology of the person who uses debt in order to achieve his goals. He sees his time span as relatively limited. He doesn't believe in the possibility of building up a family capital base over several generations. At most, he thinks that he has one lifetime in order to succeed, in order to establish his name in the eyes of the world. Therefore, he will burden himself with lots of debt in order to take advantage of special opportunities which are "the opportunities of a lifetime," but what he really means is that they are opportunities of only one person's lifetime. Thus, the gambler and the debt-burdened speculator are willing to "go for broke." And very often that is precisely what they do: go broke. They risk everything on the big deal. They try to make one big killing in life, and what usually happens is that, financially speaking, they get killed.

Autonomy and Judgment

There are many reasons why long-term debt is prohibited by the Bible. The main reason is the one that we have already discussed: the debtor is servant to the lender. Men are to be servants to God, not servants of other men.

There is a second reason. Men are not God. Men do not know everything. They cannot see into the future with great clarity. They certainly cannot see into a distant future with any kind of clarity at all. One of the best ways to have a great laugh at the experts is to go back and look at what the experts predicted twenty or twenty-five years earlier. Such predictions are an exercise in futility. Hardly anyone does anything except make a fool of himself in retrospect if he attempts to predict that far into the future.

This means that an individual who indebts his personal future beyond seven years, and perhaps even his children's future, in order to secure a present asset, is asserting an ability on his part which God says that he does not have. He is saying that he can see into the future so clearly that he knows what he is going to earn in the future, how much money he is going to have left over after all of his expenses are met, that he will not be fired, and there will not be a depression. Therefore, he will be able to repay that debt on schedule without having someone come in and take away the security for the loan. He is, therefore, implicitly asserting that he has almost perfect forecasting ability. The Bible says that he *doesn't* have such forecasting ability.

The Debtors' Revolt

In order to defend himself against the ups and downs of the economy, especially the downs of the economy, the debtor will join with other debtors in order to gain political control over money. The debtors have a reason to band together and to maintain the illusion that they actually met the obligations of their loans. They do this by pressuring the civil government into creating inflated, unbacked, "fiat" money. Fiat money is the State's "word-created" money which private citizens cannot by law turn in to the government and receive in exchange at a legally specified rate gold or silver or some other specified commodity. The State can print up all this money that it wants. It is unrestrained by the fear of a run on the Treasury's gold. When huge quantities of this unbacked money are spent into circulation by the State, debtors can dump this newly created money into the laps of the creditors. This is a false repayment, but it satisfies the legal demands of the debt contract.

When massive debt is indulged in across the board by the majority of the society, there follows an almost irresistible political pressure on the part of the debtors to inflate the currency. This leads to the destruction of values, the destruction of cooperation in the economy, the destruction of foreign credit, and on and on. It results, in other words, in very bad long-term consequences. It is, to put it bluntly, a form of *theft*.

Thus, if societies are to reduce the political threat of mass inflation, they must place limits on the legal ability of men to indebt themselves long term. This is one reason why Israel was required to cancel all debts in the seventh year. A thirty-year bond, whether issued by the State or a corporation, is opposed to Biblical law. So are thirty-year mortgages, although most Americans use long-term mortgages to finance their homes. The rise of mass inflation in peacetime has accompanied the rise of long-term debt.

Conclusion

What the Bible sets forth is a system of limited debt, and a warning against debt in general.

Most people are under the impression that the Old Testament had very rigorous laws, but the New Testament is merciful and has much more lax requirements. Actually, this is almost the reverse of reality. The Old Testament was much more lax than the New Testament, because New Testament believers have a great deal more knowledge. The more knowledge we possess, the greater our personal responsibility. From him to whom much is given, much is expected (Luke 12:48). Old Testament believers did not have the same kind of knowledge and opportunities that the New Testament believers have.

In Romans 13:8, we find the principle of New Testament debt: "Owe no one anything except to love one another." The Old Testament allowed short-term debt, but the New Testament warns us not to have any debt whatsoever.

God tells us not to serve two masters. He therefore tells us not to indulge in debt relationships, so that we can maintain our position as free men.

The modern world has ignored this rule, and the modern world faces economic devastation because of its rebellion with respect to debt.

We need to understand God's warning against debt bondage if we are to preserve our personal freedom:

1. There is no escape from servitude: we either serve God or Mammon.
2. The debtor is servant to the lender.
3. Christians are to serve God.
4. This service to God is manifested by our tithing to God through His church.
5. The debtor has mortgaged his future.
6. He has thereby announced that he can see the future.
7. The Old Testament limited debt to no more than seven years (Deuteronomy 15).
8. The New Testament says that we should not be in debt at all (Romans 13:8).
9. This applies to all institutions.
10. Usury is Biblically defined as *any* interest payment from a *charitable* loan.
11. Usury is *not* defined as "high interest."
12. Lending to "foreigners" is a means of bringing them under God's yoke.

13. Politically controlled money gives debtors a means of defrauding creditors and bringing them under Satan's yoke.

14. Widespread long-term debt leads to political pressures for monetary inflation.

15. Monetary inflation is a form of theft.

8

LET'S MAKE A DEAL

. . . work out your own salvation with fear and trembling
(Philippians 2:12b).

"Bad, bad," says the buyer; but when he goes his way, then he
boasts (Proverbs 20:14; New American Standard).

The third principle of a Biblical covenant is the principle of
ethics-dominion. For a man to begin to exercise dominion under
God, he must be able to present himself as a living sacrifice before
God (Romans 12:1). He must be allowed to offer himself and his
talents before God and men. In short, he should be allowed to
enter any market and offer his goods or services to consumers.
It's easy to misinterpret Paul's words. He isn't talking about
how to get into heaven. He is talking about what to do on earth
before you arrive at heaven's gate. Paul didn't say to work your
way into heaven, or to make your own works the basis of your salvation. What he said was to work out the salvation *which is yours*
with fear and trembling. He assumes that you already have received your salvation by grace through faith in the atoning work
of Jesus Christ at Calvary.
He makes himself perfectly clear in his letter to the Ephesians:
"For by grace you have been saved through faith, and that not of
yourselves; it is the gift of God, not of works, lest anyone should
boast. For we are His workmanship, created in Christ Jesus for
good works, which God prepared beforehand that we should walk
in them" (Ephesians 2:8-10). Salvation comes by God's grace; man
responds to this gift of salvation by acknowledging his eternal debt

99

to the work of Christ at Calvary; and then he spends the rest of his life doing his best to walk in the good works that God has ordained for him.

What this means is that God through His grace has saved us, but *He has saved us to work hard, to sustain ourselves, to take responsibility for our own actions, and to do good works*. In other words, it's our responsibility to work out the salvation which He has given us, and to work it out in fear and trembling. We are to understand the greatness of what we have been given, and we are to understand the greatness of what we are responsible for. We are to obey Him by obeying His law.

Freedom to Serve

For a man to begin to work out his salvation in fear and trembling, he needs a great deal of freedom to accomplish his tasks. The Christian is not to become a slave if he can avoid it. "Were you called while a slave? Do not be concerned about it; but if you can be made free, rather use it" (1 Corinthians 7:21). If an individual can gain greater responsibility, he is to do so, if he honestly believes that his skills and his abilities will enable him to exercise responsibility effectively. Thus, his goal should be to become *a free man, responsible before God* for his own actions, and the beneficiary of whatever productivity that he brings before God.

This means that the individual, if he is serious about serving God, should take advantage of any freedom offered to him. He does so because he can become a better servant of God, exercising greater dominion, than if he were simply doing the bidding of another individual. He is able to act on his own knowledge, in terms of his own skills, and in terms of his goals. A Christian who is mature in the faith is the best judge before God of his own capabilities, and in order to motivate him to perform at maximum productivity, he is to be given his freedom, so that he can become the beneficiary of his own efforts.

A civilization which permits hard-working, future-oriented, and thrifty individuals to work out their own salvations with fear and trembling is a society which will be the beneficiary of the collective efforts of these productive citizens.

Slaves of the State

In contrast, we have the government-controlled socialistic society which places many restrictions on what men can do for a living, when they can do it, and how much they'll be allowed to receive for the performance of their duties. It also imposes lots of paper work and other kinds of official requirements on people, who are required to report constantly to superiors who have no direct economic incentives ("take-home bonuses") in the performance of those under their authority. Productive people have to spend more time filling out forms than they do dreaming up creative ways to serve the consumer.

One of the reasons why Western society over the last two hundred years has had more rapid economic growth than any society in history is because men have been left free before God to do their best, and to serve God and man in the way that they felt they could best serve them, given their own limitations of skills, limitations of money to invest, and limitations of vision. They are also allowed to keep the fruits of their labor, their foresight, and their cost-effective planning. In short, they are allowed to *profit*.

By allowing individuals to compete in an open marketplace, with each man doing his best to serve the needs of consumers, Western society has taken advantage of the skills of hundreds of millions of individuals—individuals who probably would never have made the effort to refine their skills and abilities had they remained slaves of the State, or slaves of other individuals.

The basis in the Bible of free labor, meaning legally free labor, is the doctrine of the personal responsibility of each man to exercise his occupation, meaning his calling, before God. Because each man is told to work out his salvation with fear and trembling—to become responsible for his own life and sustenance—the State is required by God to avoid telling people how they are to bargain contractually with other people.

When we allow men to serve as free men in the marketplace, we are thereby affirming a system in which each man has an opportunity to prove his ability to his fellow man. Each man has an opportunity to come before any other man and offer to exchange his goods or services at a price which he thinks is beneficial to both parties.

This doesn't mean that the State should allow immoral behavior to go on without any punishment. What this does mean is that if a particular occupation is lawful before God, the State shouldn't legally interfere with the agreements made by men in their voluntary dealings with one another. It means simply that I can come to you and say, "I'll make you a better deal than any of my competitors will make." I should have the legal right to bid. My competitors should have that same right. This is the meaning of competition.

Buyers and Sellers

Years ago, I was in the back yard of a friend of mine who is a very successful businessman, Robert Tod. He is a graduate of the Harvard Business School, and he was (and remains) a senior partner in an extremely successful multi-million dollar business that buys up other businesses. He was talking with his four-year-old son, and he was trying to explain to his son why fathers have to go work. "Why do I have to go to work every day, Robbie?" Robbie, at age four, had a very good answer: "In order to buy money." His father replied, "No, Robbie, not to buy money—to *earn* money."

At that point I intervened. "No, Robbie is right. You go to work to buy money." The four-year-old didn't have a Harvard degree, but he had a better explanation of why his father went to work than his father did. His father thought about it for a moment, and then admitted that Robbie was correct.

We say that we earn money. That's a figure of speech. We *buy* money. When we sell our labor services, we buy money.

On the other hand, the buyer of labor services is selling money. Clearly, there is a buyer and a seller in every transaction. In any voluntary exchange, each of us is at the same time a buyer and a seller. Because of conventional speech, we don't think of it this way, but that really is the nature of the transaction.

We always forget that *every buyer is a seller,* and *every seller is a buyer.* We always say that the seller (of goods) is the person who controls the transaction. We say this because we have been taught this. Actually, the "seller" doesn't control the transaction, because *both* individuals are sellers. One person sells goods or services; the other person sells money.

Competition

Who is competing against whom in a voluntary economic exchange? Usually, we think of the buyer as competing against the seller, by which we mean that the *buyer of goods* is competing against the *seller of goods*. But in most cases, this isn't true. True enough, in a face-to-face society in which only barter is going on, there is some truth to this concept of the seller competing against the buyer. The narrower the market, the less knowledge of possible choices the buyer has, since he isn't a specialist in market demand. He is probably at a competitive (knowledge) disadvantage in comparison to the seller. But in a modern free market society, there are millions of buyers and many sellers. Sellers don't compete against buyers. Sellers compete against sellers, and buyers compete against buyers.

If I go into a store and offer to buy a particular good, and I offer the seller less money than he has on the price tag, I still may be able to buy it. If it's getting close to tax time, or if some problem has arisen in his business, the store owner may be willing to sell me the good at less than the price tag says. (The salesman may not risk it, unless I'm in an automobile dealership.)

But in most cases, the owner will refuse to make the sale. Why? Because he expects *some other buyer* to offer him the price he has put on the price tag. Furthermore, he doesn't want the word to get around that he's willing to negotiate for everything in the store, because he will wind up spending all of his time negotiating prices instead of selling. In a modern free market society, the price tag sets the terms of the deal. Because the terms are fixed and therefore *predictable*, this leads to more sales, more consumer satisfaction, and more profits for the business.

Sellers: The seller is competing against other sellers. The seller is worried that I'm going to go in, see his goods, and decide the price is too high. I may walk across the street and buy a similar but cheaper good, or the same good at a lower price. So the seller of goods is in competition with other sellers of goods.

Buyers: At an auction, I'm a buyer of goods with my money. I'm in direct competition with other potential buyers of goods with their money. The auctioneer decides who gets the goods by seeing who will bid the highest price. Simple: high bid wins! We see clearly in the case of an auction that the auctioneer is *not* in competition with the buyer. He's only trying to get greater competition *among* the buyers. He uses all the skills he has in order to increase the competition among the buyers. Buyers compete against buyers.

What if the auctioneer starts the bidding at a price above what any of the bidders are willing to bid? He isn't going to make a sale. He will be forced to lower the starting price, or put the item aside and hope that at some other auction, he may be able to sell it at a higher price.

This concept of competition is different from what you normally read about in a newspaper. The modern critic of capitalist society doesn't really understand how the market works. He doesn't understand what the basic principle of the market place is: namely, the responsible work of each man before God in order to meet his stewardship responsibility. He doesn't understand the concept of responsible ownership. He doesn't understand competition.

"Make Me a Better Offer!"

What is competition? Competition is my offering to make a better deal for the consumer than the consumer is able to get from some other seller of goods and services. Or if I'm the consumer, it's my legal right to offer a particular seller more money, or better terms or something that the seller wants compared to what any other buyer is willing to offer him. That's all competition is. It's the legal right to say, "Buy it from me," or the legal right to say, "Sell it to me." It's the legal right of an individual to offer a better deal to some other individual.

In a sense, what I'm asking the other person to do is to substitute my services, or if I'm a buyer, to substitute my offer for any-body else's competing offer. It's simply the process of *substitution*. The person who is being asked to make the substitution must be given an *incentive to switch*.

There used to be a popular cigarette commercial that featured a smoker with a black eye. "I'd rather fight than switch!" he an-nounced. Well, that is the buyer's choice. But sellers should always have the legal right to offer the buyer a better deal, to get him to change his mind.

What is immoral is the existing seller getting the government to keep his potential competitors from having the legal right to make a deal. The seller is saying, "I'd rather fight my competition than allow my customers to switch." He gets the government to threaten his competitors with fines or jail. It's an unfair, immoral fight.

Competitive offers enable all of us to get the best deal for our money if we are buyers of goods and services, or to get the great-est amount of money for our goods and services. What this means is that each individual is responsible for his own actions, and he is presumed to know his needs better than anybody else knows his needs. He alone is inside his own mind; a government official isn't inside his mind. He understands what his talents are a lot better than some bureaucrat understands them. He understands a lot better what he is willing to pay for something or give up in order to achieve something than some third party politician, many miles away.

If we wish to gain the greatest amount of service from each of our fellow citizens, we have to allow our fellow citizens *the opportun-ity to come to us and make us a better deal*. Freedom is simply a system of legal arrangements in which each individual has the legal right to make a better or different deal to anybody in the community.

"Serve Me; Push Me"

If I want to attract all other citizens who might conceivably *serve me* in some way as a consumer, then I have to allow anyone else to *compete against me* if I'm a seller. The freedom to sell to me necessarily involves the freedom to compete against me. This is the doctrine of free trade, also called open competition.

The problem is, we tend to say to ourselves, "All right, I really am willing to allow other *Americans* to compete against me, but I'm *not* willing to allow people in other countries to compete against me." This is precisely the same as saying, "I will allow other Americans to serve me, but I will never allow foreign producers to serve me." In fact, they are exactly the same statement. If I want foreign producers to serve me in my role as a consumer, I must allow foreign producers to compete against me in my role as a producer.

People find it very difficult to accept this incredibly obvious argument. They want to believe that they can get everyone in the world to serve them in their role as consumers, but they also want to prohibit these same people from competing against them in their capacity as producers. But you can't have one without the other.

Furthermore, if as a producer you want to be able to go and offer your goods to consumers in another country, then you have to allow the same opportunity for producers across the border to come to your clients to make a better offer.

What I'm saying is that the Bible teaches that each man has the right, legally, to work out his own salvation with fear and trembling before God and man—to work hard, manage his affairs well, and enjoy profits. The only exception would be trade between nations at war. If peaceful trade is legitimate with a foreign nation, then tariff-free (tax-free) trade is legitimate. There should be no discrimination against any peaceful nation, or any imported product: the same rate of taxation (tariffs) should apply to every import. The lower the rate of tariff (tax), the better for consumers.

We must allow every individual to exercise his skills and abilities to serve God and man as best as he sees fit, without legal interference in his ability to offer a better deal to anyone in the economy. Again, I'm not arguing that the State must allow people to make immoral offers—such as heroin, prostitution, pornography, or abortion—to other individuals, but I *am* saying that if some item or service is legitimate for a person to offer another individual, there should be no legal restraints placed on anyone else to make a competing offer.

There is no doubt that in some fields, some individuals in certain foreign nations can make better deals to consumers around the world. We think of Japanese electronics, or Japanese cameras, as classic examples. We need to remind ourselves that in 1952 or 1953, Japanese craftsmanship was a joke internationally, and the words "Made in Japan" didn't carry much weight. But we allowed Japanese producers to produce the best goods and services that they could. They got better at it, and the whole world has benefited from their efforts.

But the Japanese are not world competitors in the field of agriculture. On the contrary, they are importers of agricultural products. They are importers especially of American agricultural products. They are also importers of American timber products and other raw materials that they need. If we refuse to allow them to sell their cameras, their electronic equipment, and their automobiles to American citizens, then they can't buy dollars. If they can't buy dollars, how will they be able to buy soybeans and meat and timber and the other products that they need in order to sustain their life style?

"Deals Not Allowed!"

If we erect *import barriers* against Japanese products, we thereby automatically erect *export barriers* against outgoing American products. If we American consumers don't spend our dollars on Japanese goods, then the Japanese consumers can't get dollars to buy American goods. This is obvious, yet few voters on either side of the border understand it.

It works both ways. If they impose quotas and other restraints on what Americans will be allowed to export into Japan, then the Japanese consumer isn't going to get as good a deal. Because he isn't allowed by his government to buy American products, the American seller of goods isn't going to get access to as many yen, and we consumers will not be able to buy as many products from Japanese producers.

Look, a *tariff* is a *tax*. The foreign seller is required to pay an import duty to the U.S. government. We consumers then face higher prices for the imported good, and higher prices for American-produced competitive goods (since U.S. producers don't face as much price competition). Anyone who calls for higher tariffs is automatically calling for higher taxes. Yet U.S. voters seldom figure this out.

Let's go the full logic of tariffs and other trade barriers. If we say that the Japanese should not be allowed to export all they want to the United States, because in some way this hurts the United States, what about citizens in California not allowing citizens of Oregon or Nevada to export goods into California? What about citizens of New York not allowing citizens of Pennsylvania to export things into New York?

Let's take it one step farther. What about citizens of your city not allowing citizens of my city to export goods to your city? (Like this book, for instance.) And let's make it really ridiculous. What about anyone on my block in town not wanting to deal with any of those "outsiders" who live three blocks away? Where does such nonsense end?

Let's take it all the way down. Why do I cooperate even in my own family? Why do I want my wife to work on projects that I want to avoid? Why don't I wash the dishes, mend the clothes, scrub the floors, work in the garden, and do all of the other things that my wife does now much better than I? Why doesn't she go in and write the newsletters and write the books and do the audio-cassette tapes that I produce? It's simple: I hate to do these things. I don't do them well. I want her to do them. And she won't have to write books unless she wants to, and has some spare time.

The Bible teaches a division of labor principle. (See Chapter Nine: "Who's in Charge Here?") The division of labor must be respected. Each man has his own calling. Each man has his own skills to offer to other men. Each man has his own sacrifice that he brings before God. God tells us that we are to present ourselves as a living sacrifice before Him (Romans 12:1). But if the State prohibits us from making those offers and presenting ourselves before our fellow man as a living sacrifice in order to serve them better, and if it makes it illegal for us to make each other better deals, then the law has interfered with our ability to serve God best and to be served by other men who are attempting to serve man or God as best they can. At the very least, they are trying to serve their own self-interest, and the best way for them to do that is to make me a better deal.

It is true that some foreign nations subsidize companies that produce certain exports. Certainly the United States does (Export-Import Bank, etc.). Should we pressure the Federal government to impose tariffs against these subsidized products that Americans want to buy?

To answer, let me ask this question: If a foreign government wants to send me a check in the mail, should the U.S. government be allowed to intercept the check and tear it up? No? Well, the principle is the same. If intercepting foreign checks to me interferes with my freedom, then so does a retaliatory tariff against State-subsidized foreign goods. Eventually, sending me checks will prove to be stupid on the part of the foreign nation; then it will stop. This wastes the money of foreign taxpayers. So does financial assistance to exports. It may be good short-term politics, but it's bad economics. Eventually, foreign voters catch on. The practice stops.

Conclusion

What the Biblical principle of economic freedom requires is that each man be allowed to make honest, competitive offers to possible buyers of his goods or services. What freedom means is that I, as a *consumer*, am allowed by law to make any offer to buy goods and services at any price I think I can get them for. What freedom therefore must also mean is that I, as a *producer*, am allowed by law to make any offer to sell goods or services at any price I think I can get for them. *Economic freedom is the principle of competitive service.* Never forget what four-year-old Robbie Tod understood: every buyer is a seller, even a "wage-earner" (a seller of services and a buyer of money), and every seller is a buyer, even an "employer" (a seller of money and a buyer of services).

What freedom means is that I, as a consumer, am not allowed to force sellers to sell me their goods or services at prices I would prefer. I am also not allowed to get the civil government to force sellers to sell at prices I would prefer. What freedom means is that I, as a producer, am not allowed to force buyers to pay prices that I would prefer. I am also not allowed to get the civil government to force consumers to buy at prices I would prefer.

Economic freedom, in short, means this: my hand out of your wallet, and your hand out of my wallet, and neither of us uses the government as our agent of theft.

We need to recognize the basic principles of Biblical economic freedom:

1. People are responsible for their actions.
2. Christians should avoid slavery.
3. Each person knows his own skills and needs best — certainly better than bureaucrats do.
4. Western civilization was built in terms of self-responsibility.
5. The basis of profit in a competitive free market is service to the consumer.
6. A free market allows each seller to make any offer to consumers.
7. A free market allows each buyer to make any offer to producers.
8. Every buyer is also a seller, and every seller is also a buyer.
9. Sellers compete against sellers, while buyers compete against buyers.
10. The free market is a giant auction.
11. If I want sellers to compete to serve me as a consumer, I must allow sellers to compete against me as a producer.
12. Free trade means free trade for everyone, regardless of his geographical location.
13. A tariff is a tax.
14. An import barrier is at the same time an export barrier.
15. The worldwide division of labor increases everyone's opportunities, meaning everyone's wealth.

9

WHO'S IN CHARGE HERE?

> Now there are diversities of gifts, but the same Spirit. There
> are differences of ministries, but the same Lord. And there are
> diversities of activities, but it is the same God who works all in all
> (1 Corinthians 12:4-6).

The fourth principle of a Biblical covenant is the principle of
judgment-punishment, also called the principle of sanctions. God
is the final judge. In the field of economics, the principle is best
illustrated by the principle of *consumer sovereignty*, meaning the buyer's authority to make an offer. In economic affairs in a free market, the consumers, acting as competitive bidders in a giant auction, select economic winners and losers from among competing
sellers. With their spending, they reward some producers and
penalize others. They *exclude* some producers from business by
driving them into bankruptcy. In short, consumers *judge*, and they
judge in terms of what they want, not what producers want them
to want: products, prices, terms of payment, and so forth.

In a socialist economy, the rule is *bureaucratic sovereignty*, meaning government authority. State bureaucrats and politicians determine the economy's winners and losers. But there is no escape
from economic judgments. Judgment is an inescapable concept.
It's never a question of judgment vs. no judgment. It's always a
question of which kind of judgment, issued by which judge.

The Bible teaches us to respect the principle of the division of
labor. We are to work together as a species in order to glorify God,
each person offering his best talents in service to God first and then

111

to other men second. Together, we can produce more than if we were to work as isolated individuals. Hermits don't build civilizations.

The Division of Labor in the Church

Paul is writing in First Corinthians 12 concerning the church. He argues that the church is made up of people of a wide range of talents, but the church is nevertheless a single unified organization. "But one and the same Spirit works all these things, distributing to each one individually as He wills. For as the body is one and has many members, but all the members of that one body, being many, are one body, so also is Christ" (1 Corinthians 12:11-12). The church is made up of many people, and Christ directs them. But remember: He doesn't direct them in person. He directs them through representatives (church officers), and through their own personal knowledge of the Bible and their own personal circumstances.

Paul points out that the body needs many sorts of members, and no single member of the body can exist and function at its highest efficiency without all the other members.

> For in fact the body is not one member but many. If the foot should say, "Because I am not a hand, I am not of the body," is it therefore not of the body? And if the ear should say, "Because I am not an eye, I am not of the body," is it therefore not of the body? If the whole body were an eye, where would be the hearing? If the whole were hearing, where would be the smelling? But now God has set the members, each one of them, in the body just as He pleased. And if they were all one member, where would the body be? But now indeed there are many members, yet one body. And the eye cannot say to the hand, "I have no need of you"; nor again the head to the feet, "I have no need of you" (1 Corinthians 12:14-21).

Paul continues throughout the chapter in the same vein. (He writes on the same theme in Romans 12:4-8.) He is trying to get across the idea that *the church is a unified whole, despite the fact that it's made up of different parts which have very different functions and very different gifts.* He is promoting unity, but not at the expense of diversity. The church is therefore unified, because it has one head, Jesus

Christ, and also diversified, meaning that it's made up of numerous individuals who are very different from one another and who possess very different talents.

We now return again to an earlier theological theme, namely, the concept of unity and diversity. The Trinity is both unified and yet one God. Therefore, the church reflects this same diversity and unity. It can maintain itself as a unity because it has one God who has given one revelation to man, and members of the church are conveniently linked to this God, and are responsible to Him.

(It's interesting that the New Age movement's promoters also talk a lot about unity and diversity. But they have no all-powerful God in heaven who directs human history, nor do they have a reliable, open, publicly revealed Word of God to consult. They are imitating God's program, yet twisting it. This is what Satan has done from the beginning.)

The covenant involves hierarchy or authority (principle two), and it also involves moral standards (principle three). A covenantal structure is unified because it has one personal living head, and it's diversified because it has many individuals who are responsible to that single head. It has a program of action, because it has the revealed Word of God: the Bible. It has a final judgment in terms of its performance as a collective, for God is the Judge of collectives. We see this in the third chapter of Revelation, where John writes to a number of churches that have not performed according to God's standards, and he warns them that God will deal with them as individual congregational units, not simply as individual members.

The Division of Labor in the Economy

Probably the most famous textbook example of the division of labor in the economy is found in the first chapter of Adam Smith's *Wealth of Nations* (1776). He describes a pin-making factory. Each man has specialized machines to work with, and each machine does just one simple operation. Together, ten men back then could make 48,000 pins a day; if one man had been required to do the whole job, he probably couldn't have produced one pin a day. The buyer of pins benefits from the vast increase in productivity. Without the division of labor, none of us could afford as simple a consumer item as a pin. The product wouldn't even be offered for sale.

No one forced any of these ten workers to go to work. No one forced the buyers to make any purchases. Nevertheless, in freedom the pins were manufactured, and the consumers were benefited. Voluntary economic exchange makes clear the principle of the division of labor in the free market economy. The division of labor increases a society's per capita (individual) wealth.

Another example: consider a man with a hundred-acre farm. He will find it very difficult to work that hundred-acre farm unless he has very sophisticated equipment. Consider a man a hundred years ago who did not have a lot of sophisticated mechanical equipment. How would he work his farm effectively if he was by himself? He couldn't. It would pay him to hire an assistant to roll a log or to move heavy boulders or to do whatever back-breaking labor that would be virtually impossible for a single individual to achieve.

Men work together in peace, not primarily because they love each other, or because they respect each other's personal philosophies, or because they share long-run goals, or because they want to do each other favors, but because *it benefits both parties to cooperate* for certain periods of time in order to achieve certain kinds of goals. In other words, they subordinate their lusts to their quest for economic security, or for riches, or for whatever it is they are pursuing. The curse of the ground therefore becomes a benefit to mankind in general because it forces people to cooperate when otherwise they would not.

Profit or Loss

The division-of-labor model which God establishes for the church is similar to the model which He establishes for the economy. It's not identical, but it's similar. In the case of the church, there is no visible head, and there is no single individual who speaks the perfect words of Christ. There is preaching of the

Word, but preaching is always interpreted preaching, and it's always interpreted hearing. There is no escape from full responsibility to God, either on the part of the preachers or on the part of the listeners. At the same time, no individual is perfect, and therefore, there will always be imperfections in both the preaching and the listening.

The same thing is true in standards of performance in the market. Men are to exercise their callings before God as responsible, reliable individuals. Christ doesn't appear in person to tell us day by day or moment by moment that we're doing good jobs or bad jobs. We are nevertheless responsible to Him, in terms of what he has revealed to us in the Bible, and also in terms of whatever skills and abilities that we possess. We are to present our selves as a living sacrifice to God (Romans 12:1), but we aren't absolutely certain whether this sacrifice is pleasing to God or not in any particular instance.

Similarly, when we serve other individuals in our callings, we can never be absolutely certain that we're performing exactly as the buying public wants us to perform. We need some kind of guideline, some kind of standard ("blueprint"), by which we can evaluate whether or not we are *generally* serving the needs of our fellow man in our capacity as producers. We don't have the Word of God to compare their performance to, as we do as Christians in the church, or as parents in the family, or as officials in the civil government. But we do have a standard.

What is this standard? The standard is *profit or loss*. The profit-and-loss statement tells the individual producer of goods or services that the public has determined either that he has done a good job for them, or he has done such a poor job that they are in the process of taking him out of the business. Profit and loss serve him as a success indicator.

Success Indicator

Without a success indicator, there can be no successful long-term production. There will be only a waste of resources. Every producer needs a continuing success indicator, in order to guide his production to meet the needs of future consumers. This is what the profit-and-loss sheet provides him.

There is no personal, individual directing agent who tells the individual producer, "Yes, you have done a good job." No personal individual steps in, acting as the representative of the consumers as a whole, to tell the producer that he is doing well or doing poorly. Nevertheless, the producer does have a guideline. It's through a numeric unit, meaning the amount of profit as registered in terms of a monetary unit (dollar, pound, mark, yen, etc.), that he governs his business. His profits tell him clearly whether he is serving consumers efficiently or not. The producer can look at his account books and know whether he is wasting resources.

At the end of the month (or whenever), he tallies up his costs, and then compares them with his income. In this way, he discovers whether his efforts have been profitable. He makes decisions about whether or not to continue to offer his goods for sale at present prices, styles, and so forth. His profit or loss tells him about the past success or failure of the business, and this helps him to make forecasts and decisions concerning the future.

Cost-accounting makes possible the widespread division of labor. This means that people who, Biblically speaking, are the equivalent of the eye, can cooperate in a productive way with people who are the equivalent of an ear. The feet can cooperate with hands. In other words, because of the possibility of fitting together everybody's plans by means of market competition and what economists call "resource substitution" (trading one thing for another), the competitive free market provides a way for people to call forth and then combine the different talents that each of us possesses, and to do this in a way that doesn't waste resources. The market also allows consumers to influence what is going to be produced and at what prices.

Eyes and Ears Together

Because eyes can concentrate on being eyes, and feet can concentrate on being feet, the economy as a whole winds up with clearer vision and stronger feet. This means that each of us can concentrate on developing his own special skills, and profit by offering these highly developed special skills to consumers in the marketplace. This enables each of us as a consumer to call upon men throughout the economy to serve us in their capacity as specialized producers. We become the beneficiaries of the highly specialized production skills of thousands, and even hundreds of thousands, of producers.

A society couldn't operate if everybody wanted to be a professor of economics. A society couldn't operate if every member of the society wanted to do precisely the same task in life. The church would be equally devastated if everyone wanted to perform the same service within the church. This was Paul's message in 1 Corinthians 12. He was calling upon each member of the church to perform his own service as a God-fearing individual who is under the authority of Christ, so that every member of the church would become a beneficiary of the specialized skills of all the other members. This same principle operates in every organization, and especially in the free market.

The competitive free market therefore provides a means of combining the many different specialized talents of all producers in the economy. It does so by offering consumers the sovereign power of entering the market and influencing producers to serve consumers. This is a system which we call consumer sovereignty. The consumer pays, and therefore the consumer determines what gets produced next time. The old slogan, "He who pays the piper calls the tune," describes very well the system of consumer sovereignty in the free market.

The development of double-entry bookkeeping in the fourteenth century in Italy was one of the most important developments in the history of the world. It's through double-entry bookkeeping that businessmen can calculate the success or failure of their endeavors. They can tell whether certain aspects of their business are profitable, or whether they ought to be radically changed or even eliminated. Without the success indicator of modern accounting, it would be impossible to manage the modern capitalist economy.

Readers should recognize why the profit-and-loss system operates for business in much the same way as church courts operate for the church. The business is not guided by a formal appeals court hierarchy, the way the church is. Nevertheless, business does have guidelines, just as the church has the revealed guidelines of the Bible. The business operates in terms of a unity, even though it may have many people working for it.

Consumer Sovereignty

Why do consumers rule in a free market economy? Because they have the money. They earn it as producers by serving consumers; as consumers, they reward or punish producers. The rule of success is clear: *serve the consumers*. If you don't, they will take their business (their money) elsewhere.

The means of control which consumers possess is the profit-and-loss system. Remove this, and you remove the authority of consumers to offer incentives to producers to serve consumer interests. This is why bureaucratic socialist societies are centralized. They substitute the rule of government officials for the rule of the consumer. They give a few chosen officials the legal right to offer rewards and punishments. Thus, producers begin to serve the demands of these few central planners.

Consumers then lose their authority in the economy. They are almost powerless to replace the bureaucrats. They can no longer "vote" with their wallets to reward one producer over another. By abolishing profit and loss in a competitive free market, the socialists centralize economic power into their own hands. It is initially the triumph of politics over economics; then it becomes the triumph of bureaucracy over politics.

Who are the losers? Everyone except (1) the favored producers who are chosen by the bureaucrats to receive government financial aid and (2) the officials who provide this aid. Who finances this system? Consumers as taxpayers. They are compelled to finance their own destruction as sovereign consumers.

When people vote for programs of socialistic wealth redistribution, they condemn themselves to slavery. God will not be mocked. When they voluntarily abandon their role as sovereign judges of the economy, they are then judged by the bureaucratic planners who promise always "to act in the interest of the People." Instead, the bureaucrats act in their own self-interest, but with money confiscated from the voters. Voters have therefore voted away their freedom as consumers.

Conclusion

It's the division of labor which makes possible the mass production of the modern world. It's the competitive market system which integrates the plans of all the individuals, so that maximum productivity can be achieved, and consumer demand can be satisfied most efficiently.

Individuals are responsible before God for the administration of whatever assets they have been delegated, and therefore they have to make the initial decision about what should be done with these assets. They take their own knowledge, their own skills, their own abilities and their own perception of what the market requires and they must work to the best of their abilities to meet market demand. This is not a lawless system just because there is no central planning agency.

Then who serves as the judge? Consumers do. In our capacity as consumers, we tell each other in our capacity as producers just what we want to buy. And since almost all of us are producers, and almost all of us are owners, we have authority on the one hand to determine what gets done, and we have responsibility on the other hand to see that to the best of our ability it gets done. Either you serve the wants of consumers or you go bankrupt.

What the doctrine of dominion teaches, therefore, is a doctrine of *representative government*. This doesn't apply only to civil government but to *all* forms of government, whether family, church, State, business, charity, healing, education, or whatever. There is no single authority, no single chain of command. There are *multiple authorities*, and people are to be *responsible agents* before God and before men for all that has been entrusted to them.

When the State asserts the kind of authority that only God can rightfully assert, we find the rise at the same time of tyranny at the top and resistance and disruption at the bottom, as people seek to thwart the State and to thwart the planners. Modern socialism is therefore a system of *planned chaos*. It's the society of Satan, the disorderly one.

The principles undergirding the Biblical principle of the division of labor in a free market economy are these:

1. No society can operate without judges.
2. In economic affairs, either consumers are the judges or State officials are.
3. The Trinity is at the same time one and many, unity and diversity.
4. The church is a unified body having many members who possess unique gifts.
5. The church can achieve as a unit what its individual members could never achieve as individuals.
6. The free market is an institutional arrangement which brings together many participants.
7. They can achieve together what they could never achieve as individuals.
8. Sinners cooperate in the market because it is in their self-interest to do so, even when they hate each other. This increases peace.
9. The division of labor overcomes scarcity, including the scarcity of accurate knowledge.
10. Cost accounting is the integrating device by which producers make economic judgments.
11. Consumers "vote by spending" in a free market.
12. Consumers are sovereign in a free market; they serve as the judges.
13. A market open to new competitors, stable money, and profit and loss: these are the trio that grants sovereign control to consumers.
14. When consumers voluntarily vote to elect politicians who promise to steal from others, they place themselves in slavery.
15. Under socialism, self-serving bureaucrats would inherit the earth, if God were to allow socialism to continue.

10

THE LEGACY OF KNOWLEDGE

The fear of the Lord is the beginning of knowledge, But fools despise wisdom and instruction. My son, hear the instruction of your father, And do not forsake the law of your mother; For they will be graceful ornaments on your head, And chains about your neck (Proverbs 1:7-9).

The fifth and final principle of a Biblical covenant is the principle of inheritance-continuity. We might also call it the principle of legitimacy.

What is the most important inheritance a parent can leave to his children? The Bible is clear: the fear of God and the knowledge of God's precepts. As the author of Ecclesiastes (who was probably Solomon, the compiler of the Proverbs) says at the end of his book, "Let us hear the conclusion of the whole matter: Fear God, and keep His commandments, For this is the whole duty of man. For God will bring every work into judgment, Including every secret thing, Whether it is good or whether it is evil (Ecclesiastes 12:13-14).

This is why Psalm 119, the longest chapter in the Bible, is devoted entirely to the law of God. This is why parents are commanded to instruct their children in the law, from morning to evening: "And these words which I command you today shall be in your heart; you shall teach them diligently to your children, and shall talk of them when you sit in your house, when you walk by the way, when you lie down, and when you rise up" (Deuteronomy 6:6-7).

If knowledge is the most important thing that parents can

transfer to their children, then we should recognize the importance of any institutional arrangement which increases the available knowledge of society. What I argue in this chapter is that it is the free market, above any and every other ownership system, which increases both the quantity and quality of knowledge in society.

The economic questions that we need to deal with are these:

1. How do we get from personal ignorance to social (corporate) knowledge?
2. Who determines which are the most important goals, short run and long run?
3. How are men to be organized together in order to achieve these goals?
4. How is information concerning their success or failure to be transmitted to them, day by day?
5. What kinds of incentives should be offered to get men to revise their plans whenever necessary?
6. Who decides how much each person is worth in the overall production process?
7. Who tells the reward-offerers whether their judgments are correct?

How Little I Know

Years ago, Leonard Read asked this question of the president of the largest pencil manufacturing company in the United States: "How do you make a pencil?" The man initially thought it was a trick question. It wasn't. It was one of the most brilliant questions ever asked in the history of economic thought. Read proved his point by asking him a series of perfectly reasonable questions:

Do you know enough to dig the carbon and refine it, in order to make the "lead"?

You will need wood. How do you plant trees, cut them down, and transport them? With chain saws and trucks? How do you make a chain saw or a truck? Or the materials that go into chain saws and trucks?

How do you paint the pencil? With a paint machine? Fine; then how do you make the machine? How do you make the paint?

Do you know how to plant rubber trees and harvest the crop? Do you know how to vulcanize rubber? No? Then your pencil will have no eraser.

What about the metal ring that attaches the eraser to the wood? What can you tell me about metallurgy?

The president of the company then admitted that if Read wanted to put it that way, he didn't have the slightest idea how to make a pencil. Neither did anyone at the company. All they could do was buy the nearly finished ingredients that go into pencils and assemble them.

The fact is, *nobody on earth knows how to make a pencil*. Yet pencils are cheap . . . even pencils with erasers. This is the miracle of the division of labor. This is also the miracle of the free market. Together we can produce what nobody by himself knows how to produce.

But if nobody knows how to make even a pencil, think of all the other things that no single person knows anything about. We are all blind men by ourselves. Yet today we enjoy more knowledge (though probably not more wisdom) than any society in history. We therefore live like kings of old. In fact, we live *better* than kings of old.

A middle-class man with a cheap home computer has better, cheaper, and faster access to all sorts of information today than whole teams of scientists had as recently as 1960, or even later. How have we done it? More important, how do we "put it all together" into bite-size, "brain-size" packages of useful information? If we know so little as individuals, why are we so smart as a civilization?

Overcoming Ignorance

In Chapter Nine, I presented the case for the vast increase of productivity that the division of labor offers to mankind. I discussed why the free market's system of rewards and punishments, profit and loss, is the best arrangement for increasing personal productivity by means of the division of labor. It helps us to overcome scarcity.

But I only hinted at an even more important aspect of the division of labor: the division of *intellectual* labor. It isn't simply physical labor that's involved; it's also mental labor.

As individuals, we all possess highly specialized knowledge. We all have certain unique information, unique viewpoints, unique perspectives by which we view the world. Men are not all-knowing, either individually or as a species. We can never know everything (not even in heaven). Only God knows everything. Therefore, one of the ways that men can increase the total knowledge which can be brought to bear on any particular subject or problem is by *cooperative mental labor*. In other words, there is a division of intellectual labor.

Prices Are Signals

The most important institution ever developed by man for putting to use in the best way the division of intellectual labor is the competitive free market. Because of the information that prices provide in a competitive market, people can make judgments about the true conditions of supply and demand. Prices are signals. Prices are information. Without them, we are flying blind.

Who controls prices? *Consumers*. It is through their competitive bidding that resources are pushed and pulled through the economy. The high bid wins. Consumers compete against each other in the free market, and the result is a wide variety of prices. *Consumers competing against each other in the free market have collective authority over prices*. They set the economic goals of the overall economy, and their means of mutual competition, competitive money bidding (the *auction principle*), produces the technical means by which they control producers: *market prices*.

As producers, people can decide what it is that would be most profitable for them to produce, given their particular skills and resources. As consumers, they are given information about what is the best price available in order to achieve their goals. In other words, the price system and the profit-and-loss system reduce waste (increase efficiency) in the society. It makes men more efficient stewards. They don't waste as many of their own assets, which means that they aren't wasting God's assets.

The free market enables knowledge to be brought to bear on millions of problems, even though that knowledge could not be organized by any single planning agency. We don't know what is inside other people's heads. We don't know how to motivate them to search the very depths of their being to come up with solutions. We don't know, as central planning agents, how it is that we can mobilize all of this knowledge that mankind, as a whole, possesses.

Mobilizing Knowledge

Then how do we mobilize—organize and make available for our personal use—the required knowledge? Not by central economic planning, but by allowing individuals to take the initiative, to be creative in coming up with better products and better ways to do things in order to make profits. We encourage *the production and voluntary exchange of specialized knowledge*. We do this by enabling people to come into a competitive market and offer goods and services for sale, or offer money to buy goods and services.

In short, *we allow them to buy and sell ideas*.

Through the competitive bids of buyers and sellers, the market provides information to all the participants—information which could never have been located under any other type of ownership system, because even the sellers did not originally recognize the importance (and value) of all of the knowledge that they possessed before the market revealed what other people were willing to pay for it. They would not have had a full incentive to apply themselves to any particular problem.

The free market, therefore, is the primary means available for overcoming scarcity, including the scarcity of knowledge. The Book of Proverbs says that we must get wisdom (chapters 1-9). This can be done, of course, by the study of books, or by the study of the Word of God, but wisdom is also a matter of experience and the exercise of good judgment. It takes years of competition to understand a market, at least for most people. To develop the skills of good, efficient judgment, not to mention good and righteous judgment, it takes many years of study, many years of competition.

What the competitive free market allows us to do is to get the very best of men's productivity into the marketplace, so that we can sort out who does the best work, who is worthy of imitation, who should be copied, and what line of production is the most important. We could not have known this in advance. It is *only* the existence of a competitive free market which enables us to find out what the potentials are of other men and other approaches to a problem, and to find out what kinds of goods and services might be offered.

The Reconciliation of Individual Plans

Because each individual, whether acting as a consumer or as a producer, asserts his will and demonstrates his abilities in the marketplace, and because his performance is evaluated by the market by means of profit and loss, people can work out their plans logically. Nevertheless, there is no single *earthly* unified plan, as if there were a single physical planner present in the production process. On the contrary, the plans of acting individuals are very often in opposition to each other. Nevertheless, through the competitive action of the free market, the competing plans of each acting individual can be reconciled in a productive way through market competition.

Buyer and Seller

When a buyer and seller come together, they may have very different goals in mind. They may have very different plans. Because they can compete with one another, and because they can bargain with one another, and because each of them can search out someone else who may be able to be substituted for the person in front of them, there is a possibility open for the working together of these various plans.

Both the buyer and the seller want to make a deal. If they enter into a voluntary exchange, then each person has done so expecting to be better off. They both expect to win. There is no "equality of exchange." Each one thinks he will be better off after the deal is completed. In a free market, one person doesn't win at the expense of another.

The Bible is explicit about this. When buyer and seller bargain together, either may complain about what a terrible thing he is suffering. "It is naught, it is naught [bad, bad], saith the buyer: but when he is gone his way, he boasteth" (Proverbs 20:14). "Woe is me," he cries, until he gets out of earshot; then he tells his buddies what a fabulous deal he got.

In short, when buyers and sellers make a deal, each expects to be better off.

Now, each person is making predictions about the future. These predictions may not come to pass. We are human; we don't know the future perfectly. One person may think that the price of an object is going up in the future, so he wants to buy now. Another person may think that the price of that object is going down in the future, so he wants to sell now. They can get together and make a transaction, each acting in terms of his best knowledge, and while one of them will be incorrect, the market still gets the benefit (information) of the decisions of each of them.

The best information that everyone has is brought to bear on the operations of the market, and as a result of all of these competing plans and views of the future, the free market allows the efficient (low waste) working together of everyone's plans.

This doesn't mean that everybody will always be pleased with the results. We make mistakes. Some people lose money, while other people make money. Some people have their plans rewarded with profits, and other people have their plans rewarded with losses. The point is, *there is a continual process of rewards and punishments in the free market*. Good ideas or good plans are rewarded with profits, and bad ideas or bad plans are rewarded with losses. Therefore, throughout the day, or throughout the fiscal year, planners get feedback from the market—*feedback from consumers* which tells them whether or not they should pursue their present line of production.

In short, *the free market is a self-regulating system for maintaining consumer sovereignty,* meaning the authority of the buyer. It is based on the principle of *service to consumers.*

Who Else Could Make (and Enforce) the Plans?

If consumers are not sovereign in the market, then some other administrative agency must issue to the producers the plans of production for the next month, year, or decade. If consumers do not rule as directors of the processes of production, then some other agency must do it. There's only one other agency that can do it: the State. Specialized bureaucratic planners issue directives to producers, and then later hold those producers accountable for everything that they have done and all the resources they have used.

There is no escape from the production of plans, nor is there any escape from *a system of information and incentives* which sees to it that producers abide by the particular plan. There must be *revisions of plans* whenever the plans don't meet the needs of those who issue the plans in a capitalist system. But in a socialist system, there may not be any revision of plans until the entire economy crashes or slowly dies out.

In a capitalist economy, on the contrary, consumers have a legal right to change their minds, and producers either conform to the shift in taste or else they go bankrupt. In a socialist economy, producers meet the plans of a planning agency, not the direct demands of consumers. They either conform to the requirements of the central planners, or else they are fired . . . or worse.

In a capitalist economy, consumers are in charge. In a socialist economy, bureaucrats are in charge. Question: Who best represents the true needs of the society?

Representation

The economic question then is the question of representation. *Who best represents consumers?* Is it a politically elected government which in turn hires specialized bureaucratic planners to design plans and watch over production, or is the consumer best represented by the profit-and-loss statement of the individual business?

Do consumers best represent their interests as *voters*, or do they best represent their interests as *spenders*? Should their representation be politically indirect, through the ballot box, or should it be economically indirect, through the businessman's profit-and-loss statement?

It's clear that in a decentralized free market, it's the profit-and-loss statement which binds together all the talents of all the individuals who are attempting to produce in order to meet the needs of consumers. The only other alternative is for a handful of government officials to make decisions — officials who may be thousands of miles away from the consumer's decision-making in a particular store on a particular afternoon.

How good is the information possessed by bureaucratic planners three or four thousand miles away? It isn't comparable to a company's profit or loss, either as an incentive or as accurate information concerning consumer tastes. Consumers are satisfied when businesses have the best information concerning their needs, and have an incentive system which forces them to conform their productive efforts according to the information provided by the consumer. When we are talking of the *accuracy of information*, and when we are talking of the *strength of the incentives*, nothing integrates the decisions of acting individuals better than a profit-and-loss statement.

Furthermore, who is to say that bureaucrats really act as the representatives of consumers? Isn't it a lot easier to believe that they act as representatives of their own best interests? Who enforces discipline on the bureaucrats? In a socialist State, how do consumers rapidly and effectively enforce their will on the planners? At the next election? But what if the bureaucrats have lifetime jobs? What if they use their knowledge of bureaucratic rules to thwart voters? In short, *who polices the economic police?* Who rules the rulers?

The genius of the free market is that it allows us to make decisions that benefit us even if we are members of a political minority. We need 50% plus one vote to win a political election. We only need money to "win" the election at the supermarket. We get what we want when we buy; we seldom get what we want when we vote — especially eight months later, after "our" candidate has won.

Never forget Stan Evans' Law: "When our friends win the election, they aren't our friends any more."

What we have in a free market economy is the integration of many plans and many talents of many participants. Unity arises out of diversity. The freedom of individuals to pursue their own callings before God results in a system of maximum production, and maximum consumer sovereignty, because of the existence of money, and the existence of profit-and-loss statements that accountants can present to business owners who make the plan. Money is, in fact, absolutely necessary in a high division of labor economy.

What is the function of the civil government in regulating an economy? Primarily, it is to punish fraudulent or violent practices and thereby reduce the number of such practices. It establishes the rules of competition, and it enforces these rules. It is to conform itself to the Biblical blueprints regarding civil government, and in the field of economics, it is to honor the principles of labor, free trade, competitive bidding, and to enforce voluntary contracts. It is also supposed to ensure honest weights and measures (honest money). If all participants know the rules in advance, they can then make their plans accordingly.

Conclusion

We are told by God that we must increase our knowledge. We are to seek knowledge. And we are to transfer knowledge and the skills of searching for more knowledge to our children.

To obey God, we must therefore teach our children to respect the law of God. We must teach them to abide by the laws of ownership, the laws against coveting and theft, and the law of inheritance. If we do this, we shall transfer to them the moral and legal foundations of the most important source of new knowledge ever developed in man's history: the free market economy.

The free market is the institutional arrangement which offers men incentives to bring to their fellow men the best knowledge they have. The free market allows each of us to buy and sell our talents, including our intellectual talents, to anyone who wants to deal with us. The market also gives us a method of sorting out consumer-satisfying information from overpriced information. This is the system we call profit and loss.

If we fail to understand why the free market is our greatest source of new information, under God, and if we fail to teach our children to respect the Bible's laws of ownership, then we will disinherit our children. They will curse us for wasting their inheritance from God.

We need to understand these principles concerning the gathering and inheriting of economically valuable knowledge:

1. Each individual, on his own, probably does not have enough personal knowledge to keep himself alive.

2. We all depend on the division of intellectual labor to sustain us.

3. Each person has something to sell, and each person has needs to fill.

4. We communicate to each other impersonally, through the free market.

5. Prices are the means of registering the information needed by consumers and producers.

6. The plans of competing individuals are integrated and adjusted by market participants by means of profit and loss.

7. The free market allows consumers to be represented on profit-and-loss sheets.

8. Profit and loss serve as incentives for providing more and better solutions.

9. Profit and loss serve as devices for filtering out "wheat" from "chaff." The "wheat" is consumer-satisfying information.

10. People have competing goals and competing plans for the future.

11. The system of incentives in an economy should encourage plan revisions that satisfy consumers.

12. The system of incentives should represent consumers as closely as possible.

13. Socialist economies represent the interests of bureaucrats,

not consumers (or the bureaucrats' interpretation of "true" consumer needs).

14. Someone or some system must rule the rulers.

15. The free market makes consumers the rulers: they gain more direct influence through "voting by spending" than by ballot-box voting.

CONCLUSION

I have introduced some important topics of economic theory by way of the Bible's covenant structure. This covenant structure has five parts:

    1. God's transcendence (absolute difference from and sovereignty over man), yet also His immanence (constant presence with man)

    2. Authority-hierarchy (man's chain of command structure under God)

    3. Ethics-dominion (God's authoritative laws over man that give man power when obeyed)

    4. Judgment-punishment (God's promised judgments and man's judging activities)

    5. Legitimacy-inheritance (God's system for man's inheritance)

I have tried to show that all five concepts are inescapable. Every society must adopt these Biblical covenantal principles, or else imitate them. In economics, these principles translate into the following applications in relation to God:

    1. Ownership: original and delegated
    2. Authority through obedience
    3. Prohibitions against theft
    4. Scarcity as a curse-blessing
    5. World conquest through obedience

The Bible teaches that God is the Creator and Sustainer of the universe. The Bible also teaches that only God is both all-knowing

133

(omniscient) and present with the creation (omnipresent). This places the Bible in total opposition to all forms of compulsory State socialism. Modern socialism claims for the State what the Bible claims only for God: *omniscience* (perfect knowledge). Modern socialism also transfers to the State a degree of power which the Bible says belongs only to God: total power. The total power of the State is a necessary and inevitable aspect of total planning. Socialist theory therefore requires the omnipotence of the State.

The Bible teaches that only God can be regarded as a reliable central planner, because He is the Creator and heavenly Sustainer of the world. He alone possesses perfect knowledge and total power. Whenever these two aspects of God's Being are transferred to any human institution, the end result is tyranny. In the case of economics, the end result is also economic chaos, the loss of productivity, and increasing misery for everyone who isn't a high official in the State.

The Bible sets forth social requirements that can only produce a capitalist economy. It is not simply that Christian ethics agree with capitalism's ethics; rather, it is that Biblical Christianity can lead only to a society which is necessarily capitalistic. Capitalism is the historical product of Christianity, and where capitalism is abandoned, the judgment of both God and the consumers will be visited upon the economic order. Men will seek ways to hide what they already own instead of producing even more. The only winners will be the State planners, and only for a few generations, until the spiritual and economic capital of that society is eroded and destroyed.

The socialist understands implicitly that the heart and soul of modern capitalism is the private ownership, profit-and-loss system. Where profit and loss exist within the framework of the private ownership of the means of production, and when civil government does not interfere with private enterprise, consumers can flourish and prosper, if that is their goal. Yet this system stands as a testimony against all assertions that the State or any other representative agency of power possesses the characteristics or the capacities of God Almighty.

Whenever the free market is abandoned, meaning whenever the State interferes with the profitability of honest business, we find an elite corps of men asserting their own wisdom over God's: *the sovereignty of man*. This is the religion of humanism. What this really means is the sovereignty of central planning man, the new predestinator, the new god.

Power must be decentralized, the Bible teaches, whether it is political power or economic power. The best means of the decentralization of economic power is the private ownership of the means of production, and the governing "carrot and stick" of profit and loss.

Without the private ownership, profit-and-loss system, producers fly blind, and consumers are unable to assert their desires in the marketplace. Without private ownership, consumers lose their sovereignty. Any attempt of the civil government to interfere with private ownership of the means of production, or to interfere with the free market's competitive system which results in profit or loss for competing producers, inevitably reduces consumer sovereignty, and thereby reduces personal wealth.

When the State interferes with the operations of the market, it transfers power to itself. When men seek to expand the power of the State in order to steal other people's wealth, either directly (taxation) or indirectly (regulation), they create a kind of Frankenstein's monster. The State becomes the ruthless new master, replacing the sovereignty of consumers. By seeking to defeat the market, voters reduce their own freedom and therefore reduce their personal wealth. God will not be mocked. Violate His ethical standards, and you will receive judgment. The welfare State is a violation of His ethical standards. We are about to receive judgment.

The welfare State becomes the bastard inheritor. The welfare State wastes the inheritance of the society. The Biblically required program of man's dominion under God is cut short, as men seek to evade the State or manipulate the State rather than conquer the curse of scarcity through greater output. Socialism and the welfare State therefore *decapitalize* society. Socialism thwarts the dominion process.

The economies of the modern world are all welfare States. They tax their citizens at four to six times the ten percent tithe that God requires. The entire world economy is debt-burdened on a historical scale never seen before. Inflation has become a way of life. Prosperity is threatened by a looming series of catastrophes, some of which are economic, though not all. How do we escape? How do we convince God that we are sorry? What is the godly plan of restoration?

And if society ignores such a plan, what should we do as Christians to prepare for Biblical reconstruction on the far side of an economic collapse?

Part II
RECONSTRUCTION

11

FAMILY RESPONSIBILITIES

> When you sit down to eat with a ruler, Consider carefully what is before you; And put a knife to your throat If you are a man given to appetite. Do not desire his delicacies, For they are deceptive food (Proverbs 23:1-3).

In our century, families have "sat down with the ruler," the State. They have enjoyed the State's many delicacies: "free" education, "free" retirement benefits, "free" medical care, and "free" everything else. Families have been gluttons at the State's table. They have stuffed themselves with deceitful meat. Now they are suffering indigestion.

If something isn't done about it, they will become totally dependent on the State, at precisely the point in history when the State is about to go bankrupt because everyone is demanding more than it, or the taxpayers, can fulfill. What can be done to liberate families from this dependence? Christian reconstruction. What is Christian reconstruction? It's a total restructuring of programs like welfare in terms of God's revealed laws, which are found in the Bible.

There are two basic principles of politics that must be understood well in advance of any program of Christian reconstruction:

1. You can't beat something with nothing.
2. Authority flows toward those who take responsibility.

This is a book on Biblical economic principles. Readers might expect me to argue that what we need to restore a free market economy is a political revolution—a revolution in people's thinking about politics. I have adopted a different strategy.

What we have learned for three generations is that people have lost faith in private voluntary action to solve their economic problems. There has been a steady transfer of people's faith away from family, church, business, and charitable institutions and toward the civil government. There has also been a shift of faith away from local civil government to national.

This shift of faith has constituted a revolution. At bottom, it has been a *religious* revolution. It has been the substitution of the top-down bureaucratic State for the bottom-up Biblical republic. It has been the substitution of force for volunteers, taxation for the tithe, bureaucratic action for personal responsibility, and political power for personal morals. It has been the substitution of the society of Satan for the kingdom of God.

Paul wrote to Timothy: "But if anyone does not provide for his own, and especially for those of his household, he has denied the faith and is worse than an unbeliever" (1 Timothy 5:8). What Satan and his human followers have taught inside the "best" churches, "prestige" seminaries, and "fully accredited" Christian colleges is that the modern State should be forced to take on the responsibilities of providing charity. They have persuaded Christian people to betray their faith and their inheritance by calling upon the State as the agent of family welfare.

The Welfare State's Assault on the Family

I have argued throughout this book that the Bible teaches that authority is to be spread over many institutions: a system of *multiple hierarchies*. Men are to live under multiple levels of authority, all of which are under the overall sovereignty of God. The Bible teaches the world under God's grace (common and special), and the world under God's law. The Bible places the management of property under no single institution, but under several: individual, family, business, church, civil government, voluntary association, school, etc. *No single institution should possess absolute power*, and this includes economic power.

I have also argued that the primary welfare institution in society is the family. Parents are to protect, educate, and support young children. Older children are to protect their parents when the parents grow too old. There are *mutual responsibilities* as well as *mutual benefits*.

Socialism is generally defended as a war against business. It is this, of course, but it is not primarily this. Socialism is primarily a war against the family. It is the family which is the target of the transfer of responsibility: State-financed "neutral" education, State-financed charities, State-financed retirement programs, and State-financed medicine. With each new welfare program, the politicians transfer responsibility to the bureaucrats, and with every increase of State responsibility comes an increase of State power.

The State isn't doing all this as a favor. It's doing it for political and ultimately religious reasons. The central planners want to take over the role of God in people's thinking. The State, not God, will protect them. The State, not God, will educate them, employ them, exercise power over their employers, establish the terms of trade. The State becomes the final court of appeal. The State becomes the new God of world civilization.

Who represents the people before this "god"? The politicians. Who is this "god"? The central planning bureaucracy. Who "tithes" to this "god"? The people who fall down before it and pay taxes to it.

But today's golden calf isn't even made of gold. It's made of paper money, checks, and computer blips.

Recapturing Family Sovereignty

There is only one way to gain legitimate authority: *godly service*. There is only one way to redirect the flow of political power away from the State: *by taking responsibility*. If we want to see an alternative to State welfare, we must voluntarily begin by taking back the responsibility of welfare. (See George Grant's book in this series, *In the Shadow of Plenty*.)

Whenever we challenge this or that welfare activity of the State, our opponents ask us: "What would you do, let people starve?" Clearly, nobody is starving in Western industrial nations. We haven't seen starvation in the West since the Irish potato famine in the late 1840's. The answer to the threat of starvation is *economic freedom*.

Where are people starving today? In socialist and communist nations. Who feeds the Soviet Union? The West (mainly the United States, Canada, and Australia). How do we get food? By freeing up agriculture, by allowing farmers to produce whatever they want at competitive free market prices. Communist China freed up agriculture to a limited degree in 1983, and China became a net exporter of food by 1984. In short, remember this fundamental economic rule:

"You can't redistribute it, if there ain't any.

Yet there is always the nagging fear that the free market isn't enough to feed everyone. That's what the Bible says, too. There is a need for charity. But the Bible never says that the State should feed people free of charge. That's what the Roman emperors said, the rulers who persecuted the early church. Their religion was the religion of bread and circuses. Their politics was the politics of the welfare State. Their religion was salvation by politics. They persecuted Christians, for Christians believed in another Savior, Jesus Christ.

Families need to begin to pull away from the various State programs that enslave them. First and foremost, they need to reassert their belief in the future by stopping abortions. The future of the family in the West is being killed off by abortionists. Families should devote time and money in a political campaign against abortion, but also an economic campaign to help unwed mothers and married mothers to find ways to finance the birth of their children.

The next step is education. No Christian family should allow its legal dependents to enter any government-operated school. Christians are not to "tithe" their children to the State. They are to finance their children's educations in a private Christian school. Non-Christian parents should also send their children to Christian schools, but if they refuse, then at least they should send their children to private schools. The State pays for "free" education in order to capture the minds and votes of the next generation. Christians have no excuse: they must immediately pull their children out of humanistic, State-financed schools. (See Robert Thoburn's book in this series, *The Children Trap*.)

The third step is for families to take over the retirement function. Social Security is a political lie, a statistical monster which will not pay off to those who are entering the work force today, and probably not for anyone under age 50. It is a huge tax scheme which is now the number-two source of tax revenues for the United States government. It's going bankrupt. Everyone knows this today — even economists (who are usually the last to find out anything practical).

If older people have believed this lie, and have become economically dependent on Social Security checks, then they must immediately acknowledge that *they have sold themselves into slavery.* They should try to go back to work. The money from Social Security should then be donated to some charity. (Never return a government check to the government if it's owed to you by law: the bureaucrats will only use it to buy more support from someone else.) If possible, and at considerable pain, Christians must remove themselves from dependency on the State. We call drug dependence "addiction." That's exactly what Social Security is: *addiction to the State.*

The fourth step is for families to begin supporting their older members who need care. This is what the fifth commandment requires: honoring parents financially (Exodus 20:12).

The fifth step is for families to train their children in the principles set forth in the Biblical Blueprints series. They need to train up a generation of Christians who will not be compromised by the man-worshipping State.

The sixth step is for families to get out of debt. This increases their independence. They can take greater responsibility, and more profit-seeking chances, if they owe no one anything (Romans 13:8).

Christian families must begin to pay for the "free services" that the State has been providing. Until there is an answer to that question, "Would you let people starve [stay sick, stay uneducated, stay poor, etc.]?", we cannot expect voters to vote out of existence the welfare State. Until Christian families become responsible, no one else will.

In short, you can't beat something with nothing.

If the Present System Continues

God will not be mocked. Societies that defy Him by breaking His laws are eventually placed under His judgment. These judgments are very frequently the outworking of the original sins. In the case of the welfare State, it goes bankrupt.

The bills are coming due. The U.S. government is running annual deficits of over $200 billion. This can't go on forever. It probably can't go on until the year 2000. Either we balance the budget, or we pay off the debt with inflated money. Most nations historically have paid off their debts with inflated money.

If the present welfare State isn't reversed by the appearance of voluntary charities and family responsibility, then the voters will continue to increase their economic dependence on a socialist system which is clearly, unmistakably, and steadily going bankrupt. The U.S. deficit is so large today that if 100% of all net new wealth created by the U.S. economy were devoted to financing the deficit, it would still be at least $110 billion in the red. (Figure it out: 3% economic growth after inflation times a $3 trillion economy produces $90 billion; $200 billion minus $90 billion is $110 billion.)

We know where the numbers are headed, yet we continue to "play pretend." We play games. We pretend that national bankruptcy isn't just around the corner—even assuming the Third World doesn't default on its debt to Western banks.

What we will find when the day of financial reckoning comes is that overnight, practically everyone will lose his "connection" to his "habit." People's dependence on the State will not be able to be sustained. The wealth of the taxpayers will not be able to support the continued growth of the bureaucracy.

At that point, most families will learn the hard way that *there is no such thing as a free lunch*. They will learn that addiction eventually destroys the addict. They will see their guaranteed retirement go down the drain of mass inflation. They will see their public school systems bankrupted, the schools' buildings and facilities falling into irreversible disrepair. Wherever they have become dependent on the State, they will suffer losses, possibly total losses if they have no independent financial reserves.

If this happens, they will also see *revolution*. The question then will be: Who will win?

The Need for Immediate Action

There is very little that families can do politically to reverse the drift toward the economic waterfall. The problem isn't primarily political; the problem is religious. It will take a moral revolution to reverse the public's faith in the State. This faith is wearing thin, but most people simply refuse to believe in an alternative. They will hang onto the welfare State's drifting rowboat until it goes over the falls.

To pull back from disaster in time, there has to be a revival. But not just another "feel good and get into heaven, too" sort of revival. I mean a drastic reversal of today's humanistic, State-worshipping world-and-life view, which most Christians passively accept (or at least vote in terms of). I mean a revival so huge that professors in Christian colleges actually stop assigning humanist textbooks to their students, and start teaching their subjects in terms of what the Bible actually demands.

Mind-boggling, isn't it? We've never had a revival that powerful. But we need one. Soon. That's what the Biblical Blueprints series is all about: the restructuring of every area of life in terms of the Bible. These books will anger a lot of professors at Christian colleges. They will anger a lot of politicians. They will anger a lot of businessmen who are "on the dole" from the State, and families that are also dependent on State welfare. But that's what revival is all about: confronting people with their sins, and showing them God's way of escape.

Eventually the addict either suffers the agony of withdrawal from the drug, or else he dies. The question for every Christian family is this: *How can I reduce my dependence?* How can I become a responsible person? The answer must begin at home, and it must begin immediately. Families must not continue to search for some other agency to finance their endless desires at below-market prices. They must not continue to believe that some loving government official is going to solve their problems free of charge. They must forever abandon faith in that endless promise: "I'm from the government, and I'm here to help you."

If the government ever publishes a book to show bureaucrats how to serve the public, it will be a cookbook.

Conclusion

There is no escape from responsibility. Christians are now in a position to serve as examples to the families of the world. They need to begin to get their houses in order. This includes economic order.

Families need to prepare for the worst. When God brings judgment on this civilization, those who have confidence in a sovereign God and His reliable principles of righteous action will possess the courage of their convictions. They will be in a position to lead.

Today, things seem to be bumping along rather well. Few people believe that they need God. They are like the fools described by God, fools who have said in their hearts: "My power and the might of my hand have gained me this wealth" (Deuteronomy 8:17). They have placed their faith in the State; they have placed their futures in the hands of God-despising humanist bureaucrats. They will suffer the terrible consequences.

Christians dare not share this faith in the State. They must turn to God and His eternal principles of righteous action as their source of success. They must not become modern versions of the Israelites in the wilderness who worshipped a golden calf that their leaders had constructed for them. They must begin taking the steps necessary to get as far away from modern calf-worship as they can, accepting no more hand-outs from its priests, the bureaucrats.

12

CHURCH RESPONSIBILITIES

I know your works [Church of Laodicea], that you are neither
cold nor hot. I could wish you were cold or hot. So then, because
you are lukewarm, and neither cold nor hot, I will spew you out of
My mouth. Because you say, 'I am rich, have become wealthy, and
have need of nothing' and do not know that you are wretched,
miserable, poor, blind, and naked . . . (Revelation 3:15-17).

Churches today, like every other institution, are rich beyond
the wildest dreams of men a century ago. The vast outpouring of
productivity which the free market has produced since the late
1700's has transformed all of us. By historical standards, we are
fantastically wealthy.

Yet the church is miserable, poor, and blind today, just as the
Church of Laodicea was in John's day. It is neither hot nor cold. It
has lost its impact in society. In the liberal camp, the churches
can't compete against revolutionary groups, or liberal politics, or
just evening television. In evangelical circles, the churches can't
compete against the large television ministries, called the "electronic church," or just evening television.

Conservative fundamentalist churches are growing, and a minority of these churches have tentatively begun to experiment
with social action projects (mostly the abortion issue), Christian
schools, and politics. So far, they have not begun to have much
political impact, and certainly not much economic impact, in the
community at large, especially outside the South and rural
Midwest.

The church is not to become the primary agency of welfare.

The family is. The church is to *guard* the family, however. If families get into trouble financially, the church is to intervene and see what can be done. Paul called upon the church at Corinth to raise money (2 Corinthians 8) to assist the poverty-stricken families in Jerusalem (1 Corinthians 16:3). If families are headed for financial trouble, church officers are to intervene and provide guidance.

The Tithe

The church is entitled to the tithe, or ten percent of after-tax family income. This has been true since the days when Abraham paid his tithe to Melchizedek, the high priest of Salem (Genesis 14:18-20), which later became the city of Jeru-Salem. Because churches no longer preach this requirement of the tithe consistently, they have not been able to redirect the flow of authority in their direction. Authority flows in the direction of those institutions that bear social risks and take responsibility. The churches have not called upon their members to make available the funds that God says His church is entitled to. The churches, like the families, have thereby transferred power to the State.

The tithe is built into man's affairs. Either we pay it to the church, or we will pay it to the State. The church limits its lawful demands to 10%; the State will extract all it can get. The modern welfare State demands far more than the tithe. The combined level of taxation of all branches of government in the United States exceeds 40% of all national income.

This is sinful. It is also the judgment of God on rebels. It happens every time men rebel against the tithe. The taxes of Egypt in Joseph's day were only half of this, or 20% (Genesis 47:24). The prophet Samuel came before the Israelites and warned them that the king they wanted would eventually take 10% of their wealth: "And he will take the tenth of your seed, and of your vineyards, and give to his officers, and to his servants" (1 Samuel 8:15).

Christians live in a country that extracts four times the tithe from them, and they vote for politicians who promise even more government spending. They are in bondage, but they fail to recognize it. They are in Egypt, but they fail to recognize it.

A Program of Reconstruction

The first step that churches need to take is to require that each voting member, or head of household, pay 10% of his after-tax income to the church. "No representation without taxation." This will force men to take seriously the responsibilities of full membership. It will also force them to come to grips with the importance of the church as an agency of welfare.

Second, churches probably should take at least 10% of their income from people's tithes and offerings and set this money aside for welfare activities. They should care for the poor, or work with local churches that have ministries to the poor. This is how churches can pay tithes.

In the Old Testament, there was a special poor tithe at the end of every three years. The poor, the foreign residents, and the Levitical priests were to be invited to a national feast of celebration (Deuteronomy 14:22-29). The money was used to finance every family in the land in a special celebration before God. Some commentators believe that every third year, the entire tithe was set aside for the poor. Others think it was one-third of the tithe every year. The closest celebrations to this that we have in the United States are the annual turkey dinners at Thanksgiving and Christmas, when poor people ("bums") are given a free meal at the local rescue mission. The steadily employed members of the community never show up. It is not a true communal celebration.

Question: Why don't churches do this? Why do parachurch or non-church ministries do it?

Third, churches should see to it that the wife of every head of household has sufficient low-cost "term" life insurance written on her husband's life to protect her and the children. She should own the policy, paying for it from her own personal, exclusive checkbook. This establishes her as the owner of the policy.

Why should she own it? First, it does not become part of his estate, so there is no inheritance tax involved. Second, what if he quits the church, divorces her, and remarries? If he owns the policy, he will probably name the new wife as the beneficiary, leaving the first wife without alimony income if he dies. If necessary, her husband can give her the money for the premiums. Thus, if he dies, the wife is protected, and the church is not bankrupted trying to support her.

There is a fine home budget program for computers written by Andrew Tobias. It is called "Managing Your Money." It sells for $200. You can buy it at half price from several discount centers, such as 47th Street Computer, in New York City. This program has several excellent features that help families get a grip on expenses. The best feature is a life insurance estimation section. It asks the husband basic questions: number of children, how long until they are on their own, age, wife's needs, expected rate of return on the proceeds of the policy, and so forth. The husband tells the program what he wants, and it tells him how much term insurance he needs to achieve his goals.

I have never seen any man under age 40 whose wife didn't need (according to his own criteria) at least $500,000. You can only get this with term insurance. And you can get it incredibly cheap! In some cases for under $400 a year.

Term insurance is simple: if the insured person dies, the company pays the beneficiary. It is easy to calculate the cost per thousand dollars of insurance: divide the face value of the policy by the annual premium. A person 35 years old should pay less than $2 per thousand. One firm that sells low cost term insurance is Old Line Life Insurance, Milwaukee, Wisconsin. Another is Kemper Insurance Co. Deacons should see to it that every wife has this protection.

What if the family is really poverty-stricken? What if they really can't afford $200 a year for basic protection? In that case, the deacons need to step in and give the wife enough money to meet the annual premium payment to the insurance company. This relieves the congregation of the threat of having to support the widow and children if the husband dies. The deacons are acting in the name of God, the wife (who needs the protection), the husband (whose responsibility it is to protect her), and the congregation (which also needs protection).

Fourth, the church should see to it that each family has adequate health insurance. The church becomes responsible if there is an accident, and the families are impoverished because of medical costs. The church therefore has a legitimate police function to make sure that each member has adequate health insurance coverage. Again, if the family is very poor, the church should pay for the premiums until the father gets back on his feet financially.

Fifth, churches should assist non-church ministries that specialize in aiding the poor: hospitals, Good Will-type groups, rescue missions, and so forth. Let those who better understand the needs (and "hustles") of the poor administer the funds.

Sixth, churches should set up scholarship funds for poor families inside the church, and a few for families outside the church. Economically speaking, and in terms of what churches are supposed to be doing, this is much better than setting up actual church schools. (Because of state controls on education, church-run schools may be a way of creating more temporary protection for Christian education, but a church-run school should be a last-gasp effort. Christian education should be independent of church control, and one group of members should not be asked to finance the educations of children of middle-class members by creating a school with below-cost tuitions.)

Seventh, churches should see to it that families are providing care for aged parents without relying on the State. This doesn't mean that families should bankrupt themselves in order to get parents off of Medicare or out of public housing, but they should be cutting family expenses to the bone in an attempt to reassert their responsibility for their parents. For example, anyone who is wealthy enough to own his own home, or have financial equity in it, has no excuse for accepting State aid, either for himself or his parents. To accept such welfare payments is to create a dangerous dependence on the State, and to affirm the religious belief in the modern State as savior.

Eighth, pastors should preach regularly on the topic of church responsibility to the poor. They should also make it clear that such teaching is in open opposition to the modern doctrine of the State's responsibility to the poor. They must call for a replacement operation, not a church-financed supplement to the modern welfare State. Anyone who preaches for more private charity without *also* calling for a reduction in tax-financed charity is a guilt-manipulator and an accomplice to the socialists.

Ninth, poverty programs must be accompanied by preaching and instruction concerning the moral responsibility of the able-bodied to work. Paul wrote, "If anyone will not work, neither shall he eat" (2 Thessalonians 3:10b). The world doesn't owe any able-bodied person a living. Neither does God. *To financially aid laziness is to financially aid evil.* The long-term goal of all poverty programs should be to make the recipients financially independent.

Modern socialistic poverty programs are just that: *programs for extending poverty.* Aid to dependent children has become aid to immoral unwed mothers. There are now third-generation welfare check recipients in every welfare State. Rome had similar programs in the era of the early church. These programs bankrupted the Empire financially, but Rome had been bankrupt morally long before. The proof of this moral bankruptcy was the existence of the politics of bread and circuses. It is no different today.

Tenth, pastors should teach the Biblical principles of financial success: self-discipline, thrift, hard work, customer service, thrift, future-orientation, saving for retirement, thrift, profitability, low or zero debt, thrift, long hours, family sacrifice, reduced lifestyle, and thrift. They should prepare their people for the worst, so the people will be capable of handling the best, when it comes.

Churches need to train their members in the theology and specifics of Christian dominion, in every area of life. We are supposed to inherit the earth. In fact, we *have* inherited the earth. But we have not yet occupied it. We have not yet established authority. Adam inherited the earth before he sinned and gave it away, but even in his sin-free state, he had to take possession of his inheritance. He received title, but he didn't receive it completed.

Through Christ, we have inherited the earth. We, too, must now take possession of our inheritance. We have title, but we have not been given occupancy. That takes a program of dominion.

If the Present System Continues

The church's self-imposed impotence, *its refusal to take responsibility*, has made possible the rise of the welfare State. Liberal theologians have applauded this turn of events, while conservative Christians have grumbled a lot but have done nothing institutionally to fight it.

Let us assume that the system continues. It will be anti-business as usual. Taxes will remain high, the Federal deficits will continue, and eventually the politicians will bail out the system with monetary inflation. The State will hide its bankruptcy by creating money.

We will have a series of devastating financial crises, just as Rome had after the year 200, and just as France had just before and during the French Revolution (1785-1795). Inflation will destroy people's faith in the government, and will make it difficult for families to keep up.

When these crises hit, the churches will be subject to economic pressures that they have not seen since the Great Depression of the 1930's. Giving will drop unless members are highly self-disciplined (and even church-disciplined). Members will lose jobs, or find their savings wiped out. The poor will multiply. This time, unlike the 1930's, the State will have tapped into every known source of taxable income. There will be no State-financed "safety net" next time.

Which groups will be ready to offer support by being willing and able to organize and make available charity? Which groups will have prepared their members for the risk-taking and responsibility-bearing that are needed for survival in an economic crisis? Who will be ready to lead?

Conclusion

The churches are just barely getting ready to consider such a shift in responsibility, let alone a shift in authority. If revival comes alongside the economic crises, as I would expect, then church leaders have to be ready to answer the fundamental questions:

1. How did the world economy get into such a mess?
2. What Biblical economic principles were violated, 1913 to the present?
3. How do we return to Biblical economic principles?
4. Who should finance reconstruction?
5. What should I do with my money?
6. What should I do if I lose my job?
7. How can I afford to tithe?

Pastors and deacons are almost completely unprepared to take leadership today. No one really expects them to. They are considered unnecessary by most people. After all, the Bible-believing church has had little or nothing to say about economic issues throughout this century. Economics has been considered "off limits" to preachers in conservative churches.

This will change, and it will change fast, when the crises hit. At that point, those who begin to exercise responsibility will position themselves as leaders in the national and perhaps even the worldwide transformation which may lie ahead. Churches had better begin now to preach God's principles of success, and God's principles of *responsible* giving.

13

STATE RESPONSIBILITIES

> You shall do no injustice in judgment. You shall not be partial
> to the poor, nor honor the person of the mighty. But in righteous-
> ness you shall judge your neighbor (Leviticus 19:15).

The civil government possesses a monopoly: the monopoly of
violence. It alone has the right to inflict fines, physical punishment, and death on those who violate the laws of God and those
statutes written by men in conformity to God's legal principles.

The problem is, this monopoly of violence can be misused.
Men from the beginning of time have sought political power in
order to control their personal rivals. They have used violence
against their competitors, all in the name of justice.

The result has been an ever-increasing State. Each group
wants special economic favors from the State: direct financial aid,
as well as indirect financial aid: taxpayer-financed insurance from
loss, restrictions in trade for competitors (and therefore consumers), higher rates of taxation for rivals, State-granted professional
licenses that exclude rivals, tariffs and quotas against foreign-
manufactured goods, price "floors" (in agriculture, this scheme is
called "parity") that make voluntary bargaining illegal, price "ceil-
ings" that make voluntary bargaining illegal, and on and on. Each
scheme is advocated as a necessary exception to the general principles of economic freedom. Each one is promoted in the name of
"the public interest." Each one involves the theft of money, freedom of choice among alternatives, or future innovations.

(I guarantee you, a substantial percentage of my readers are

155

thinking to themselves right now: "Well, I agreed with North up until now. But he's gone too far! He's challenging the perfectly proper right of the State to regulate the sale of [my product or service]. This whole book is therefore nonsense." Note: if you're thinking this to yourself, the State has already captured your life, your mind, and your future. You are in moral and intellectual bondage, for you presently exist in terms of the State's *temporary and conditional* grant of an economic monopoly to your occupational special-interest group. You will be asked to pay for this special financial aid, one way or another. There are no free lunches in life. The State isn't here to help you free of charge.)

Each group tries to impoverish its competition. Inescapably, all consumers are harmed at the same time. What the seeker of benefits wants is to keep consumers from working out a deal with his competitors at a price that he is unwilling or unable to match. He regards such deals as unfair competition. You can imagine what buggy whip manufacturers would have done to Henry Ford, if the State had been bigger back then.

I can remember a political campaign in the 1960's in California to prohibit pay-per-show television. The existing "free" television stations succeeded in getting a proposition on the ballot to outlaw pay T.V. (Maybe it was the other way around; I forget. Maybe the pay T.V. promoters were somehow required to get a bill passed in order to be allowed to offer their services for sale.) The "free" T.V. stations waged a propaganda war in the newspapers against this "unfair" new source of entertainment. I remember especially a full-page newspaper advertisement which showed a child in front of a T.V. He was asking his father why his father wouldn't pay to allow him to watch a show.

This was a blatant appeal to the fear of financial loss on the part of parents, meaning lower-middle-class and poor parents. Freedom of choice was ignored. Benefits to adults were ignored. Today, as we have learned, parents are the people who watch subscription T.V., since most programming is aimed at adults. I think the "free" T.V. industry knew that back in the 1960's, too. But the voters approved the initiative; pay T.V. was outlawed in

California for over a decade. Voters kept the "rich" from enjoying the service; they also kept themselves from enjoying it.

Pay T.V. is now beginning to erode the government-granted (Federal Communications Commission-licensed) monopoly of "free" T.V. This was what free T.V. feared a generation ago. The monopolists wanted a hammerlock on the consumer. This is what government restrictions on trade are all about. It's not a question of monopoly vs. no monopoly when it comes to government-mandated restrictions on trade; it's a question of *who gets* the monopoly.

The Loss of Freedom

As the State grows, it gains support for even further growth by promising benefits to its supporters. It promises offsetting financial grants that will supposedly make up for losses to those who are being abused by the existing State-created monopolies. It is a never-ending competitive struggle for control over the granting of monopolies.

And behind every monopoly is the ultimate institutional monopoly: *the legal monopoly of violence.*

The problem for justice-seekers is that as men lose their freedoms, they become increasingly dependent on their master, the State. They want more and more. After all, at a below-market price for anything, there is greater demand than supply. The State offers "free" services. There will be heavy demand for them. The State has told people that they have a "right" to these "free" services. Now the voters are demanding "rights"—a lot more potent appeal than simply a request for a hand-out or political pay-off.

The State finds that it cannot afford to defend the nation and provide justice when it has to feed the hungry, clothe the poor, house the homeless, and give a college education to every semi-literate student who wants to stay out of the labor force for a few more years. So the politicians take the path of least resistance: they buy the votes of the irresponsible. They try to walk away from the State's God-assigned responsibilities in the few areas that

God has assigned to it: national defense, civil justice, public safety, and medical quarantine.

Whenever self-government under God and God's law fades, the State must pick up the slack. There are no "responsibility vacuums." When the State buys off the voters with promises of State-guaranteed safety, citizens become increasingly irresponsible. They are trained to search for someone else, or some other institution, to take responsibility for their weaknesses and mistakes.

This is contrary to the fundamental principles of Christian dominion. It is the attitude which says, "Someone else made me foul up." This was Adam's response to God in the garden: "The woman whom You gave to be with me, she gave me of the tree, and I ate" (Genesis 3:12). It was Eve's response to God, too: "The serpent deceived me, and I ate" (3:13b). As comedian Flip Wilson has his character Geraldine say, "The Devil made me do it!" In short, *"It was your fault, God, for making my environment so difficult!"*

It wasn't God's fault. It was man's fault. Man is fully responsible for his own actions, before God and before other men. He is eternally responsible before God. Rebellious man hates the thought of this. He wants to deny it. So he seeks a State which allows him to deny it. He seeks a State which can save him from his guilt, his responsibility, and his mistakes. He seeks the Savior State.

Shrinking the State

The first step is moral and religious. It is to affirm one's own personal responsibility for one's own actions. In our day, this will take either a religious revival, or a collapse of the State so complete that each person will have no choice but to face the inescapable reality of personal responsibility. It may take both. It probably will take both.

The second step is to begin pulling away from State subsidies. Stop taking the checks. Stop sending lobbyists to Washington to get your group special favors. Send lobbyists only to reduce State controls over your industry, not increase them for others.

The third step is to begin to strengthen your commitment to

the family and the church. This means tithing. This means saving for retirement, sending your children to a Christian school, and supporting parents who are in need. Alternative institutions must be built up that will steadily take responsibility for the welfare "services" the State has taken upon itself.

Fourth, it means getting involved in *local* social action. This may begin with picketing an abortion clinic. It may mean picketing stores that sell pornography—yes, even "soft-core, middle-class pornography." It may begin with setting up (and financing) a crisis pregnancy center. It means *beginning*.

Fifth, these sorts of commitments should escalate to political involvement. Politics, like every other area of life, is an area of Christian responsibility and Christian dominion. But in almost all cases, this commitment should begin with *local* politics.

Localism

Christians seem to want to run for governor before they serve as dogcatchers. They want to be Congressmen before they serve as County Commissioners. They grab prematurely for the robes of authority. This is what Adam did in the garden. He wanted all knowledge, even at the expense of disobeying God. Christians want to run before they crawl.

This is not the Biblical way. We are to be trained in service at lower levels before we serve in higher levels. This is God's requirement for church officers (1 Timothy 3). It should be the normal path for civil officers, too.

We must also understand that a primary political goal is *decentralization*. Those activities that the national civil government now controls should be the responsibility of state or local civil governments. Power should be lodged closer to home. So should taxes. The national civil government is essentially an appeals court. It is to settle disputes that lower courts find too difficult.

Jethro, Moses' father-in-law, made this plain in his advice to Moses, which Moses adopted as law in Israel.

> And you shall teach them [the people] the statutes and the laws, and show them the way in which they must walk and the work they

must do. Moreover you shall select from all the people able men, such as fear God, men of truth, hating covetousness; and place such over them to be rulers of thousands, rulers of hundreds, rulers of fifties, and rulers of tens. And let them judge the people at all times. Then it will be that every great matter they shall bring to you, but every small matter they themselves shall judge. So it will be easier for you, for they will bear the burden with you (Exodus 18:20-22).

Remember that Moses had direct communication with God. He could issue perfect justice. But he was overwhelmed with the backlog of unheard cases. It was better for Israel to get imperfect justice from honest judges than to wait endlessly for an opportunity to get perfect justice from God.

Today, we don't expect perfect justice from anyone. We might as well content ourselves with swift justice from local courts.

The first step for every Christian who is elected locally is to vote against every hand-out from Washington. No more Federal money in local affairs. No more Federal control attached to that money. No more "revenue sharing" from a bankrupt Federal government that runs a $200 billion a year budget deficit. It has no revenues to share.

The local civil government is to pay its own way, make its own decisions, *and be ready to pick up the pieces after a financial collapse or major military setback*. We need alternative, *legitimate* civil governments. We need to avoid revolution. This means that we need to start taking over local government, right under the noses of the Federal bureaucrats.

Everyone wants to be in the "big time" politically. Everyone wants to run for governor. *Let them*. Meanwhile, we take over where today's politicians think that nothing important is happening. We should get our initial experience in ruling on a local level. We must prepare ourselves for a long-term political battle. We start out as privates and corporals, not colonels and generals. We do it God's way.

Vote "No"

A very simple first step in self-discipline under God is to get the State out of debt bondage. Vote "no" on every bond issue. No exceptions. The answer is "no."

Then, if you're so inclined, run for the public school board. Your job, if elected, is to say "no." Do teachers want a raise? Vote against it. Does the district want to float yet another bond issue? Vote against it. Do they want to build a new high school? Vote against it. Do they want to buy new textbooks? Vote against it.

You can do this politically in the name of the taxpayer. Ultimately, you're doing this in the name of God. He is the enemy of the public schools. They are His enemy. God wants them all shut down, with the possible exception of the nation's military academies and local police academies (where the government buys its future military leaders and law enforcement officers, both legitimate functions of the State). They want Him shut down (no prayers in the schools, no religious instruction in the schools, etc.). This is a war. You must get on God's side.

Does the city council want to build tennis courts at the parks? Vote against it. The civil government isn't supposed to be in the exercise business or the entertainment business.

Does the city want to provide more free services? Vote "no."

Vote "Yes"

I don't want to appear negative. There are lots of things to vote for. One thing to vote for is the imposition of *user fees* for every city service that isn't connected with protection of life and property, or the administration of civil justice.

Can any city service be done by a profit-seeking firm? Vote "yes." Let the city stop collecting garbage free of charge. After all, people don't get their newspapers delivered free of charge. Why should the city pay to haul them away?

If nothing else, at least let private firms bid to perform city services less expensively. The famous American race car promoter, the late J. C. Agajanian, was a member of a financially successful Armenian family that originally made its fortune by contracting to pick up garbage in Southern California. His father, J. T., operated a hog ranch in the (then) little town of Newhall, California. Local cities paid him to pick up their garbage. He fed it to his pigs, and then sold the pigs. Later on, he collected the remains of the pigs in the garbage — all at a profit. This is "economic ecology" at its best. This is the way Armenians do business: *profitably.* Should we be surprised to learn that Armenia was the first nation to adopt Christianity, decades before Constantine established it as Rome's religion? (By the way, I married an Armenian. I wanted to find out how they do it. She ran my publishing business for the first five years, the period in which most new businesses go bankrupt. Mine made it.)

Can you find any aspect of the government that could be sold to the employees and turned into a private profit center? All over Great Britain, this is taking place daily. The process is called *privatization.* This is saving the British taxpayers billions of pounds sterling each year, and it's getting them better service. The national telephone system, British Airways, British natural gas, even the airports have been privatized.

This can be done at the local level. It should be done. The function of the civil government is not to redistribute wealth from citizen to citizen. Civil government is to provide justice for all in terms of predictable, publicly available Biblical law. This is why the nation of Israel was required by God to have the law read publicly every seven years, in the year of release, the sabbatical year (Deuteronomy 31:10-13).

When governments get involved in providing "free" services, they inevitably become involved in the redistribution of wealth by force (laws) and violence. This is why it is imperative to limit civil government to providing the services that every citizen needs and is required by God to have: the protection of Biblical law, and the restraint of Biblical law.

If the Present System Continues

We are headed for national bankruptcy. It is only a question of time. It is also a question of which form the bankruptcy will take. Will it be an open declaration that "the Federal government cannot honor all of its welfare, debt, and military obligations"? Or will it be a disguised default: mass inflation, price controls, and rationing of goods and services? Will we first get another round of tax increases, especially a national sales tax (or "value added tax," the VAT)?

I predict mass inflation, followed by price controls and rationing. I call this "government by emergency." I even wrote a book with that title, with suggestions as to how families and churches can protect themselves from this form of national bankruptcy.

No State is able to imitate God successfully. No State is a savior. Salvation by law, especially State law, is the devil's own lie. This means that there will eventually be judgment on every State which has asserted near-divine status. Christians should do their best to avoid any sort of economic dependence on such a State, so that when it falls, they will not be crushed by it or dragged down by it.

All the programs will go bankrupt: Social Security, Federal retirement, the repayment of Treasury debt, the subsidizing of nearly bankrupt businesses (especially the big multinational banks), the creation of State-protected monopolies (including trade unions), and all the rest. When the State is bankrupt, it will be impotent. It will have to be trimmed back to its original God-given functions: the protection of life and property from violence.

During the crisis, Christians will be called upon as never before to exercise charity and godly dominion. At that point, we will see a massive shift of power. Power will go to those who exercise responsibility and charity, and who can show men how to put their lives back together. If it isn't the church, Christian charities, and Christian families, who will it be?

Conclusion

Christians need to begin a long-term strategy of capturing authority at every level of civil government. This will not be successful until they believe that God calls them to freedom from the State. Also, it will not be done until they have already begun to support private charities (beginning with family welfare obligations) with their own hard-earned money. It probably will not happen until the State bankrupts itself and millions of voters in a wave of financial crises that the State's own policies have created.

The goal is to *roll back the State*. The goal is to get the State's hand out of our wallets, even if it's doing so "in the name of the People." Christians must agree to this program: "My hand out of your wallet; your hand out of my wallet; and handcuffs on the thieves."

BIBLIOGRAPHY

Anderson, Digby, editor. *The Kindness that Kills: The Churches' Simplistic Response to Complex Social Issues*. London: SPCK, 1984.

Banfield, Edward. *The Unheavenly City Revisited*. Boston: Little, Brown & Co., 1974

Chilton, David. *Productive Christians in an Age of Guilt-Manipulators: A Biblical Response to Ronald J. Sider*. 4th edition. Tyler, Texas: Institute for Christian Economics, 1986.

Davis, John Jefferson. *Your Wealth in God's World: Does the Bible Support Free Enterprise?* Phillipsburg, New Jersey: Presbyterian & Reformed, 1984.

Friedman, Milton and Friedman, Rose. *Free to Choose*. New York: Harcourt Brace Jovanovich, 1980.

_____. *Tyranny of the Status Quo*. New York: Harcourt Brace Jovanovich, 1984.

Gilder, George. *The Spirit of Enterprise*. New York: Simon & Schuster, 1984.

Griffiths, Brian. *The Creation of Wealth*. London: Hodder & Stoughton, 1984.

_____. *Morality and the Market Place: Christian Alternatives to Capitalism and Socialism*. London: Hodder & Stoughton, 1982.

Hayek, F. A. *The Road to Serfdom*. Chicago: University of Chicago Press, 1944.

Hazlitt, Henry. *Economics in One Lesson*. New York: Crown, [1946].

Hodge, Ian. *Baptized Inflation: A Critique of "Christian" Keynesianism*. Tyler, Texas: Institute for Christian Economics, 1986.

Mises, Ludwig von. *Bureaucracy*. Cedar Falls, Iowa: Center for Futures Education, [1944].

North, Gary. *An Introduction to Christian Economics*. Nutley, New Jersey: Craig Press, 1973

_____. *Dominion and Common Grace*. Tyler, Texas: Institute for Christian Economics, 1986.

_____. *The Dominion Covenant: Genesis*. Tyler, Texas: Institute for Christian Economics, 1982

_____. "Free Market Capitalism," in Robert G. Clouse (editor), *Wealth and Poverty: Four Christian Views*. Downers Grove, Illinois: InterVarsity Press, 1984. Distributed exclusively by Dominion Press, Ft. Worth, Texas.

_____. *Moses and Pharaoh: Dominion Religion vs. Power Religion*. Tyler, Texas: Institute for Christian Economics, 1985.

_____. *Resurrection vs. Entropy: Crisis in the Christian Worldview*. Tyler, Texas: Institute for Christian Economics, 1987.

_____. *The Sinai Strategy: Economics and the Ten Commandments*. Tyler, Texas: Institute for Christian Economics, 1986.

_____, editor. Symposium on Christian Economics, *The Journal of Christian Reconstruction*, Vol. II (Summer, 1975), published by the Chalcedon Foundation, Vallecito, California.

Rabushka, Alvin. *Hong Kong: A Study in Economic Freedom*. Chicago: University of Chicago Press, 1979.

Roepke, Wilhelm. *Economics of the Free Society*. Chicago: Regnery, 1963.

_____. *A Humane Economy*. Chicago: Regnery, 1960.

Rose, Tom. *Economics: The American Economy from a Christian Perspective*. Mercer, Pennsylvania: American Enterprise Publications, 1985.

_____. *Economics: Principles and Policy from a Christian Perspective*. Milford, Michigan: Mott Media, 1977.

Schoeck, Helmut. *Envy: A Theory of Social Behavior*. New York: Harcourt, Brace, & World, 1970.

Shafarevich, Igor. *The Socialist Phenomenon*. New York: Harper & Row, 1980.

Simon, Julian. *The Ultimate Resource*. Princeton: Princeton University Press, 1981.

Sowell, Thomas. *Knowledge and Decisions*. New York: Basic Books, 1981.

——————. *Markets and Minorities*. New York: Basic Books, 1981.

Sutton, Ray. *That You May Prosper: Dominion by Covenant*. Ft. Worth, Texas: Dominion Press, 1987.

SCRIPTURE INDEX

OLD TESTAMENT

NEW TESTAMENT

SUBJECT INDEX

New world order, 56
Noah, 72
Nuclear Energy, 3
Nuclear power, 4

Oaths, 24
Obedience, 29
Omniscience, 19-20
Original Sin, 144
Ownership
  Biblical vs. socialist, 21
  collective and individualistic, 12
  costs, 18
  free market system and, 12
  expensive, 18
  individual, 25-26
  mutual, 82
  moral responsibility of, 20
  original, 11
  overlapping principle, 12
  private vs. collective, 20
  religious concept, 11
  social function, 14, 78
  socialistic debate, 12
  theocentric, 11, 19
  Trinitarian, 12
  voluntary, 13-14

Parable of Absent Landlord, 61
Parenthood, 83
Parents
  knowledge, 121
  responsibility, 66
Pastors, 151-152
Payne, Robert, 80n
Personal Responsibility, 26
Pharaoh, 27
Pin-Making Factory, 113
Plato, 83
Political revolt, 5, 139
Politicians, 9
Politics
  basic principles, 139

local, 159
  salvation by, 142
Pollution, 3
Pornography, 106
Poverty, 72, 152
Power
  decentralized, 72
  grabbing for, 27
  not absolute, 140
  recipients of, 78
Predictions, 127
Price
  competition, 53-54
  controls, 163
  signals, 124
Private property
  importance of, 40
  reinforced by God, 77
Privatization, 162
Process of discovery, 21
Production techniques, 54
Profit
  indicator of success, 116
  loss and, 18, 115
Profit and Loss Statement, 125
Profit-Sharing Plan, 53
Providence, 11
Property
  administration of, 3
  decisions and, 18
  family, 24-26
  human rights and, 26
  management of, 10, 140
  New Testament view of, 24
  Old Testament view of, 24
  overlapping ownership, 12
  ownership and, 38
  private, 15
  proper distribution of, 20
  rights of exclusion, 75-76
  shared, 14
Prostitution, 106

WHAT ARE BIBLICAL BLUEPRINTS?

by Gary North

How many times have you heard this one?

"The Bible isn't a textbook of . . ."

You've heard it about as many times as you've heard this one:

"The Bible doesn't provide blueprints for . . ."

The odd fact is that some of the people who assure you of this are Christians. Nevertheless, if you ask them, "Does the Bible have answers for the problems of life?" you'll get an unqualified "yes" for an answer.

Question: If the Bible isn't a textbook, and if it doesn't provide blueprints, then just how, specifically and concretely, does it provide answers for life's problems? Either it answers real-life problems, or it doesn't.

In short: *Does the Bible make a difference?*

Let's put it another way. If a mass revival at last hits this nation, and if millions of people are regenerated by God's grace through faith in the saving work of Jesus Christ at Calvary, will this change be visible in the way the new converts run their lives? Will their politics change, their business dealings change, their families change, their family budgets change, and their church membership change?

In short: Will conversion make a visible difference in our personal lives? If not, why not?

Second, two or three years later, will Congress be voting for a different kind of defense policy, foreign relations policy, environmental policy, immigration policy, monetary policy, and so forth?

Will the Federal budget change? If not, why not?

In short: Will conversion to Christ make a visible difference in our civilization? If not, why not?

The Great Commission

What the Biblical Blueprints Series is attempting to do is to outline what some of that visible difference in our culture ought to be. The authors are attempting to set forth, in clear language, *fundamental Biblical principles* in numerous specific areas of life. The authors are not content to speak in vague generalities. These books not only set forth explicit principles that are found in the Bible and derived from the Bible, they also offer specific practical suggestions about what things need to be changed, and how Christians can begin programs that will produce these many changes.

The authors see the task of American Christians just as the Puritans who came to North America in the 1630's saw their task: *to establish a city on a hill* (Matthew 5:14). The authors want to see a Biblical reconstruction of the United States, so that it can serve as an example to be followed all over the world. They believe that God's principles are tools of evangelism, to bring the nations to Christ. The Bible promises us that these principles will produce such good fruit that the whole world will marvel (Deuteronomy 4:5-8). When nations begin to marvel, they will begin to soften to the message of the gospel. What the authors are calling for is *comprehensive revival*—a revival that will transform everything on earth.

In other words, the authors are calling Christians to obey God and take up the Great Commission: to *disciple* (discipline) all the nations of the earth (Matthew 28:19).

What each author argues is that there are God-required principles of thought and practice in areas that some people today believe to be outside the area of "religion." What Christians should know by now is that *nothing* lies outside religion. God is judging all of our thoughts and acts, judging our institutions, and working through human history to bring this world to a final judgment.

We present the case that God offers *comprehensive salvation* — regeneration, healing, restoration, and the obligation of total social reconstruction — because the world is in *comprehensive sin.*

To judge the world it is obvious that God has to have standards. If there were no absolute standards, there could be no earthly judgment, and no final judgment because men could not be held accountable.

(Warning: these next few paragraphs are very important. They are the base of the entire Blueprints series. It is important that you understand my reasoning. I really believe that if you understand it, you will agree with it.)

To argue that God's standards don't apply to everything is to argue that sin hasn't affected and infected everything. To argue that God's Word doesn't give us a revelation of God's requirements for us is to argue that we are flying blind as Christians. It is to argue that there are *zones of moral neutrality* that God will not judge, either today or at the day of judgment, because these zones somehow are *outside His jurisdiction.* In short, "no law-no jurisdiction."

But if God *does* have jurisdiction over the whole universe, which is what every Christian believes, then there must be universal standards by which God executes judgment. The authors of this series argue for God's *comprehensive judgment,* and we declare His *comprehensive salvation.* We therefore are presenting a few of His *comprehensive blueprints.*

The Concept of Blueprints

An architectural blueprint gives us the structural requirements of a building. A blueprint isn't intended to tell the owner where to put the furniture or what color to paint the rooms. A blueprint does place limits on where the furniture and appliances should be put — laundry here, kitchen there, etc. — but it doesn't take away our personal options based on personal taste. A blueprint just specifies what must be done during construction for the building to do its job and to survive the test of time. It gives direction to the contractor. Nobody wants to be on the twelfth floor of a building that collapses.

Today, we are unquestionably on the twelfth floor, and maybe even the fiftieth. Most of today's "buildings" (institutions) were designed by humanists, for use by humanists, but paid for mostly by Christians (investments, donations, and taxes). These "buildings" aren't safe. Christians (and a lot of non-Christians) now are hearing the creaking and groaning of these tottering buildings. Millions of people have now concluded that it's time to: (1) call in a totally new team of foundation and structural specialists to begin a complete renovation, or (2) hire the original contractors to make at least temporary structural modifications until we can all move to safer quarters, or (3) call for an emergency helicopter team because time has just about run out, and the elevators aren't safe either.

The writers of this series believe that the first option is the wise one: Christians need to rebuild the foundations, using the Bible as their guide. This view is ignored by those who still hope and pray for the third approach: God's helicopter escape. Finally, those who have faith in minor structural repairs don't tell us what or where these hoped-for safe quarters are, or how humanist contractors are going to build them any safer next time.

Why is it that some Christians say that God hasn't drawn up any blueprints? If God doesn't give us blueprints, then who does? If God doesn't set the permanent standards, then who does? If God hasn't any standards to judge men by, then who judges man?

The humanists' answer is inescapable: *man* does — autonomous, design-it-yourself, do-it-yourself man. Christians call this man-glorifying religion the religion of humanism. It is amazing how many Christians until quite recently have believed humanism's first doctrinal point, namely, that God has not established permanent blueprints for man and man's institutions. Christians who hold such a view of God's law serve as *humanism's chaplains*.

Men are God's appointed "contractors." We were never supposed to draw up the blueprints, but we *are* supposed to execute them, in history and then after the resurrection. Men have been given dominion on the earth to subdue it for God's glory. "So God created man in His own image; in the image of God He created him; male and female He created them. Then God blessed them, and God said to them, 'Be fruitful and multiply; fill the earth and subdue it; have dominion over the fish of the sea, over the birds of the air, and over every living thing that moves on the earth'" (Genesis 1:27-28).

Christians about a century ago decided that God never gave them the responsibility to do any building (except for churches). That was just what the humanists had been waiting for. They immediately stepped in, took over the job of contractor ("Someone has to do it!"), and then announced that they would also be in charge of drawing up the blueprints. We can see the results of a similar assertion in Genesis, chapter 11: the tower of Babel. Do you remember God's response to that particular humanistic public works project?

Never Be Embarrassed By the Bible

This sounds simple enough. Why should Christians be embarrassed by the Bible? But they *are* embarrassed . . . millions of them. The humanists have probably done more to slow down the spread of the gospel by convincing Christians to be embarrassed by the Bible than by any other strategy they have adopted.

Test your own thinking. Answer this question: "Is God mostly a God of love or mostly a God of wrath?" Think about it before you answer.

It's a trick question. The Biblical answer is: "God is equally a God of love and a God of wrath." But Christians these days will generally answer almost automatically, "God is mostly a God of love, not wrath."

Now in their hearts, they know this answer can't be true. God sent His Son to the cross to die. His own Son! That's how much God hates sin. That's wrath with a capital "W."

But why did He do it? Because He loves His Son, and those who follow His Son. So, you just can't talk about the wrath of God without talking about the love of God, and vice versa. The cross is the best proof we have: God is both wrathful and loving. Without the fires of hell as the reason for the cross, the agony of Jesus Christ on the cross was a mistake, a case of drastic overkill.

What about heaven and hell? We know from John's vision of the day of judgment, "Death and Hades [hell] were cast into the lake of fire. This is the second death. And anyone not found written in the Book of Life was cast into the lake of fire" (Revelation 20:14-15).

Those whose names are in the Book of Life spend eternity with God in their perfect, sin-free, resurrected bodies. The Bible calls this the New Heaven and the New Earth.

Now, which is more eternal, the lake of fire, or the New Heaven and the New Earth? Obviously, they are both eternal. So, God's wrath is equally ultimate with His love throughout eternity. *Christians all admit this*, but sometimes only under extreme pressure. And that is precisely the problem.

For over a hundred years, theological liberals have blathered on and on about the love of God. But when you ask them, "What about hell?" they start dancing verbally. If you press them, they eventually deny the existence of eternal judgment. We *must* understand: they have no doctrine of the total love of God because they have no doctrine of the total wrath of God. They can't really understand what it is that God in His grace offers us in Christ because they refuse to admit what eternal judgment tells us about the character of God.

The doctrine of eternal fiery judgment is by far the most unacceptable doctrine in the Bible, as far as hell-bound humanists are concerned. They can't believe that Christians can believe in such a horror. But we do. We must. This belief is the foundation of Christian evangelism. It is the motivation for Christian foreign missions. We shouldn't be surprised that the God-haters would like us to drop this doctrine. When Christians believe it, they make too much trouble for God's enemies.

So if we believe in this doctrine, the doctrine above all others that ought to embarrass us before humanists, then why do we start to squirm when God-hating people ask us: "Well, what kind of God would require the death penalty? What kind of God would send a plague (or other physical judgment) on people, the way He sent one on the Israelites, killing 70,000 of them, even though they had done nothing wrong, just because David had conducted a military census in peacetime (2 Samuel 24:10-16)? What kind of God sends AIDS?" The proper answer: "The God of the Bible, *my* God."

Compared to the doctrine of eternal punishment, what is some two-bit judgment like a plague? Compared to eternal screaming agony in the lake of fire, without hope of escape, what is the death penalty? The liberals try to embarrass us about these earthly "down payments" on God's final judgment because they want to rid the world of the idea of final judgment. So they insult the character of God, and also the character of Christians, by sneering at the Bible's account of who God is, what He has done in history, and what He requires from men.

Are you tired of their sneering? I know I am.

Nothing in the Bible should be an embarrassment to any Christian. We may not know for certain precisely how some Biblical truth or historic event should be properly applied in our day, but every historic record, law, announcement, prophecy, judgment, and warning in the Bible is the very Word of God, and is not to be flinched at by anyone who calls himself by Christ's name.

We must never doubt that whatever God did in the Old Testament era, the Second Person of the Trinity also did. God's counsel and judgments are not divided. We must be careful not to regard Jesus Christ as a sort of "unindicted co-conspirator" when we read the Old Testament. "For whoever is ashamed of Me and My words in this adulterous and sinful generation, of him the Son of Man also will be ashamed when He comes in the glory of His Father with the holy angels" (Mark 8:38).

My point here is simple. If we as Christians can accept what is a very hard principle of the Bible, that Christ was a blood sacrifice for our individual sins, then we shouldn't flinch at accepting any of the rest of God's principles. As we joyfully accepted His salvation, so we must joyfully embrace all of His principles that affect any and every area of our lives.

The Whole Bible

When, in a court of law, the witness puts his hand on the Bible and swears to tell the truth, the whole truth, and nothing but the truth, so help him God, he thereby swears on the Word of God — the *whole* Word of God, and *nothing but* the Word of God. The Bible is a unit. It's a "package deal." The New Testament doesn't overturn the Old Testament; it's a *commentary* on the Old Testament. It tells us how to use the Old Testament properly in the period after the death and resurrection of Israel's messiah, God's Son.

Jesus said: "Do not think that I came to destroy the Law or the Prophets. I did not come to destroy but to fulfill. For assuredly, I say to you, till heaven and earth pass away, one jot or one tittle will by no means pass from the law till all is fulfilled. Whoever therefore breaks one of the least of these commandments, and teaches men to do so, shall be called least in the kingdom of heaven; but whoever does and teaches them, he shall be called great in the kingdom of heaven" (Matthew 5:17-19). The Old Testament isn't a discarded first draft of God's Word. It isn't "God's Word emeritus."

Dominion Christianity teaches that there are four covenants under God, meaning four kinds of *vows* under God: personal (individual), and the three institutional covenants: ecclesiastical (the church), civil (governments), and family. All other human institutions (business, educational, charitable, etc.) are to one degree or other under the jurisdiction of these four covenants. No single covenant is absolute; therefore, no single institution is all-powerful. Thus, Christian liberty is *liberty under God and God's law.*

Christianity therefore teaches pluralism, but a very special kind of pluralism: plural institutions under God's comprehensive law. It does not teach a pluralism of law structures, or a pluralism of moralities, for as we will see shortly, this sort of ultimate pluralism (as distinguished from *institutional* pluralism) is always either polytheistic or humanistic. Christian people are required to take dominion over the earth by means of all these God-ordained institutions, not just the church, or just the state, or just the family.

The kingdom of God includes every human institution, and every aspect of life, for all of life is under God and is governed by His unchanging principles. All of life is under God and God's principles because God intends to *judge* all of life *in terms of* His principles.

In this structure of *plural governments*, the institutional churches serve as *advisors* to the other institutions (the Levitical function), but the churches can only pressure individual leaders through the threat of excommunication. As a restraining factor on unwarranted church authority, an unlawful excommunication by one local church or denomination is always subject to review by the others if and when the excommunicated person seeks membership elsewhere. Thus, each of the three covenantal institutions is to be run under God, as interpreted by its lawfully elected or ordained leaders, with the advice of the churches, not the compulsion.

Majority Rule

Just for the record, the authors aren't in favor of imposing some sort of top-down bureaucratic tyranny in the name of Christ. The kingdom of God requires a bottom-up society. The bottom-up Christian society rests ultimately on the doctrine of *self*-government under God. It's the humanist view of society that promotes top-down bureaucratic power.

The authors are in favor of evangelism and missions leading to a widespread Christian revival, so that the great mass of earth's inhabitants will place themselves under Christ's protection, and voluntarily use His covenantal principles for self-government. Christian reconstruction begins with personal conversion to Christ and self-government under God's principles, then spreads to others through revival, and only later brings comprehensive changes in civil law, when the vast majority of voters voluntarily agree to live under Biblical blueprints.

Let's get this straight: Christian reconstruction depends on majority rule. Of course, the leaders of the Christian reconstructionist movement expect a majority eventually to accept Christ as savior. If this doesn't happen, then Christians must be content with only partial reconstruction, and only partial blessings from

God. It isn't possible to ramrod God's blessings from the top down, unless you're God. Only humanists think that man is God. All we're trying to do is get the ramrod away from them, and melt it down. The melted ramrod could then be used to make a great grave marker for humanism: "The God That Failed."

The Continuing Heresy of Dualism

Many (of course, not all!) of the objections to the material in this book series will come from people who have a worldview that is very close to an ancient church problem: dualism. A lot of well-meaning Christian people are dualists, although they don't even know what it is.

Dualism teaches that the world is inherently divided: spirit vs. matter, or law vs. mercy, or mind vs. matter, or nature vs. grace. What the Bible teaches is that this world is divided *ethically* and *personally*: Satan vs. God, right vs. wrong. The conflict between God and Satan will end at the final judgment. Whenever Christians substitute some other form of dualism for ethical dualism, they fall into heresy and suffer the consequences. That's what has happened today. We are suffering from revived versions of ancient heresies.

Marcion's Dualism

The Old Testament was written by the same God who wrote the New Testament. There were not two Gods in history, meaning there was no dualism or radical split between the two testamental periods. There is only one God, in time and eternity.

This idea has had opposition throughout church history. An ancient two-Gods heresy was first promoted in the church about a century after Christ's crucifixion, and the church has always regarded it as just that, a heresy. It was proposed by a man named Marcion. Basically, this heresy teaches that there are two completely different law systems in the Bible: Old Testament law and New Testament law (or non-law). But Marcion took the logic of his position all the way. He argued that two law systems means two Gods. The God of wrath wrote the Old Testament, and the God of mercy wrote the New Testament. In short: "two laws-two Gods."

Many Christians still believe something dangerously close to Marcionism: not a two-Gods view, exactly, but a God-who-changed-all-His-rules sort of view. They begin with the accurate teaching that the ceremonial laws of the Old Testament were fulfilled by Christ, and therefore that the *unchanging principles* of Biblical worship are *applied differently* in the New Testament. But then they erroneously conclude that the whole Old Testament system of civil law was dropped by God, and *nothing Biblical was put in its place.* In other words, God created a sort of vacuum for state law.

This idea turns civil law-making over to Satan. In our day, this means that civil law-making is turned over to humanists. *Christians have unwittingly become the philosophical allies of the humanists with respect to civil law.* With respect to their doctrine of the state, therefore, most Christians hold what is in effect a two-Gods view of the Bible.

Gnosticism's Dualism

Another ancient heresy that is still with us is gnosticism. It became a major threat to the early church almost from the beginning. It was also a form of dualism, a theory of a radical split. The gnostics taught that the split is between evil matter and good spirit. Thus, their goal was to escape this material world through other-worldly exercises that punish the body. They believed in *retreat from the world of human conflicts and responsibility.* Some of these ideas got into the church, and people started doing ridiculous things. One "saint" sat on a platform on top of a pole for several decades. This was considered very spiritual. (Who fed him? Who cleaned up after him?)

Thus, many Christians came to view "the world" as something permanently outside the kingdom of God. They believed that this hostile, forever-evil world cannot be redeemed, reformed, and reconstructed. Jesus didn't really die for it, and it can't be healed. At best, it can be subdued by power (maybe). This dualistic view of the world vs. God's kingdom narrowly restricted any earthly manifestation of God's kingdom. Christians who were influenced by gnosticism concluded that God's kingdom refers only to the institutional church. They argued that the institutional church is the *only* manifestation of God's kingdom.

This led to two opposite and equally evil conclusions. *First*, power religionists ("salvation through political power") who accepted this definition of God's kingdom tried to put the institutional church in charge of everything, since it is supposedly "the only manifestation of God's kingdom on earth." To subdue the supposedly unredeemable world, which is forever outside the kingdom, the institutional church has to rule with the sword. A single, monolithic institutional church then gives orders to the state, and the state must without question enforce these orders with the sword. The hierarchy of the institutional church concentrates political and economic power. *What then becomes of liberty?*

Second, escape religionists ("salvation is exclusively internal") who also accepted this narrow definition of the kingdom sought refuge from the evil world of matter and politics by fleeing to hide inside the institutional church, an exclusively "spiritual kingdom," now narrowly defined. They abandoned the world to evil tyrants. *What then becomes of liberty?* What becomes of the idea of God's progressive restoration of all things under Jesus Christ? What, finally, becomes of the idea of Biblical dominion?

When Christians improperly narrow their definition of the kingdom of God, the visible influence of this comprehensive kingdom (both spiritual and institutional at the same time) begins to shrivel up. The first heresy leads to tyranny *by* the church, and the second heresy leads to tyranny *over* the church. Both of these narrow definitions of God's kingdom destroy the liberty of the responsible Christian man, self-governed under God and God's law.

Zoroaster's Dualism

The last ancient pagan idea that still lives on is also a variant of dualism: matter vs. spirit. It teaches that God and Satan, good and evil, are forever locked in combat, and that good never triumphs over evil. The Persian religion of Zoroastrianism has held such a view for over 2,500 years. The incredibly popular "Star Wars" movies were based on this view of the world: the "dark" side of "the force" against its "light" side. In modern versions of this ancient dualism, the "force" is usually seen as itself impersonal: individuals personalize either the dark side or the light side by "plugging into" its power.

There are millions of Christians who have adopted a very pessimistic version of this dualism, though not in an impersonal form. God's kingdom is battling Satan's, and God's is losing. History isn't going to get better. In fact, things are going to get a lot worse externally. Evil will visibly push good into the shadows. The church is like a band of soldiers who are surrounded by a huge army of Indians. "We can't win boys, so hold the fort until Jesus comes to rescue us!"

That doesn't sound like Abraham, Moses, Joshua, Gideon, and David, does it? Christians read to their children one of the children's favorite stories, David and Goliath, yet in their own lives, millions of Christian parents really think that the Goliaths of this world are the unbeatable earthly winners. Christians haven't even picked up a stone.

Until very recently.

An Agenda for Victory

The change has come since 1980. Many Christians' thinking has shifted. Dualism, gnosticism, and "God changed His program midstream" ideas have begun to be challenged. The politicians have already begun to reckon with the consequences. Politicians are the people we pay to raise their wet index fingers in the wind to sense a shift, and they have sensed it. It scares them, too. It should.

A new vision has captured the imaginations of a growing army of registered voters. This new vision is simple: it's the old vision of Genesis 1:27-28 and Matthew 28:19-20. It's called *dominion*.

Four distinct ideas must be present in any ideology that expects to overturn the existing view of the world and the existing social order:

    A doctrine of ultimate truth (permanence)
    A doctrine of providence (confidence)
    Optimism toward the future (motivation)
    Binding comprehensive law (reconstruction)

The Marxists have had such a vision, or at least those Marxists who don't live inside the bureaucratic giants called the Soviet Union and Red China. The radical (please, not "fundamentalist") Muslims of Iran also have such a view.

Now, for the first time in over 300 years, Bible-believing Christians have rediscovered these four points in the theology of Christianity. For the first time in over 300 years, a growing number of Christians are starting to view themselves as an army on the move. This army will grow. This series is designed to help it grow. And grow tougher.

The authors of this series are determined to set the agenda in world affairs for the next few centuries. We know where the permanent answers are found: in the Bible, and *only* in the Bible. We believe that we have begun to discover at least preliminary answers to the key questions. There may be better answers, clearer answers, and more orthodox answers, but they must be found in the Bible, not at Harvard University or on the CBS Evening News.

We are self-consciously firing the opening shot. We are calling the whole Christian community to join with us in a very serious debate, just as Luther called them to debate him when he nailed the 95 theses to the church door, over four and a half centuries ago.

It is through such an exchange of ideas by those who take the Bible seriously that a nation and a civilization can be saved. There are now 5 billion people in the world. If we are to win our world (and these billions of souls) for Christ we must lift up the message of Christ by becoming the city on the hill. When the world sees the blessings by God upon a nation run by His principles, the mass conversion of whole nations to the Kingdom of our Lord will be the most incredible in of all history.

If we're correct about the God-required nature of our agenda, it will attract a dedicated following. It will produce a social transformation that could dwarf the Reformation. This time, we're not limiting our call for reformation to the institutional church.

This time, we mean business.

Jesus said to "Occupy till I come." But if Christians don't control the territory, they can't occupy it. They get tossed out into cultural "outer darkness," which is just exactly what the secular humanists have done to Christians in the 20th century: in education, in the arts, in entertainment, in politics, and certainly in the mainline churches and seminaries. Today, the humanists are "occupying." But they won't be for long. *Backward, Christian Soldiers?* shows you why. This is must reading for all Christians as a supplement to the *Biblical Blueprints Series*. You can obtain a copy by sending $1.00 (a $5.95 value) to:

Institute for Christian Economics
P.O. Box 8000
Tyler, TX 75703

_____
name

_____
address

_____
city, state, zip

_____
area code and phone number

Dr. Gary North
Institute for Christian Economics
P.O. Box 8000
Tyler, TX 75711

Dear Dr. North:

I read about your organization in your book, *Inherit the Earth*. I understand that you publish several newsletters that are sent out for six months free of charge. I would be interested in receiving them:

☐ *Biblical Economics Today*
   Christian Reconstruction
   and Dominion Strategies

Please send any other information you have concerning your program.

_____
name

_____
address

_____
city, state, zip

_____
area code and phone number

☐ Enclosed is a tax-deductible donation to help meet expenses.

The *Biblical Blueprints Series* is a multi-volume book series that gives Biblical solutions for the problems facing our culture today. Each book deals with a specific topic in a simple, easy to read style such as economics, government, law, crime and punishment, welfare and poverty, taxes, money and banking, politics, the environment, retirement, and much more.

Each book can be read in one evening and will give you the basic Biblical principles on each topic. Each book concludes with three chapters on how to apply the principles in your life, the church and the nation. Every chapter is summarized so that the entire book can be absorbed in just a few minutes.

As you read these books, you will discover hundreds of new ways to serve God. Each book will show you ways that you can start to implement God's plan in your own life. As hundreds of thousands join you, and millions more begin to follow the example set, a civilization can be changed.

Why will people change their lives? Because they will see God's blessings on those who live by His Word (Deuteronomy 4:6-8).

Each title in the *Biblical Blueprints Series* is available in a deluxe paperback edition for $6.95, or a classic leatherbound edition for $14.95.

The following titles are scheduled for publication in 1986:

- Introduction to Dominion: Biblical Blueprints on Dominion
- Honest Money: Biblical Blueprints on Money and Banking
- Who Owns the Family?: Biblical Blueprints on the Family and the State
- In the Shadow of Plenty: Biblical Blueprints on Welfare and Poverty
- Liberator of the Nations: Biblical Blueprints on Political Action
- Inherit the Earth: Biblical Blueprints on Economics
- Chariots of God: Biblical Blueprints on Defense
- The Children Trap: Biblical Blueprints on Education
- Entangling Alliances: Biblical Blueprints on Foreign Policy
- Ruler of the Nations: Biblical Blueprints on Government
- Protection of the Innocent: Biblical Blueprints on Crime and Punishment

Additional Volumes of the Biblical Blueprints Series are scheduled for 1987 and 1988.

Please send more information concerning this program.

---

name

---

address

---

city, state, zip

Dominion Press • P.O. Box 8204 • Ft. Worth, TX 76124